NOBODY GOES TO
JERUSALEM

THE LONG LETTERS HOME 1995

NOBODY GOES TO JERUSALEM

Ralph Alpert

Published by Rach Mi El Press, Santa Cruz,
California
PO Box 8288, Santa Cruz, CA 95061.

Photo editing and design of book interior,
cover and maps by Rebecca Barnes.

Front and back covers: *The Starting Point:
Santa Cruz, where the River San Lorenzo
meets the Sea.* Photo by Rebecca Barnes.

Back cover: painting of the author by
Gabrielle Fuchs.

Typefaces used are Century Schoolbook,
Adobe Hebrew, Minion Pro, Calibri, Roboto,
and Optima.

ISBN-13: 978-0-9995109-0-2

To Fannie and Mendel, and Beatzie

Contents

viii

Introduction

I began writing long letters home, when traveling, to several friends in the 1980s. Later, I saved the originals and mailed copies. When I returned from the trips I put the originals of the letters in a cabinet and never looked at them until a few years ago when I happened to pick up one letter and began to read it. I have already put one long letter in book form: *The Long Letters Home: The Color of Morning — 1990.*

This long letter and this book are from my trip to Israel and elsewhere in 1995. I am Jewish but had little contact with Judaism as a religion until I attended a bat mitzvah in early 1995. This led, later that year, to joining a Jewish Renewal congregation in Santa Cruz. I had a meeting set for Maine in October of 1995, and I decided to go on from Maine to Israel with the purpose of learning more about Judaism. Thus the trip, the letter, this book. (For more on my relation to Jewishness and Judaism, see *On Being Jewish*, page 215.)

⌒

Thanks to Joyce Michaelson for encouraging me to put these letters into book form. And thanks to Sunshine Gibbs, Marilyn Bosworth (the distinguished reader), Steve Bosworth, Steve Leonard, Rich Mick, Ron Rook, and the others who took part in the Tuesday Pizza and Literary Society.

My heartfelt thanks to Rebecca Barnes for her help in making this book — not only is she very competent, with lots of good ideas, but she is also fun to work with.

~ *1* ᔏ

Santa Cruz

Do I see God, whatever that is?

Santa Cruz   Wednesday, October 4, 1995, 9:26 am
Yom Kippur. I sit at my table, drink a glass of orange
juice colored dark green. It contains a tablespoon of Pro
Green, the super whammy vitamin stuff. I set out over
two hours ago, into the beautiful balmy morning, to buy a
newspaper. No — not really to buy a newspaper — really
just to walk. I bought the paper and kept on walking.
Until I reached the sea.

I stood on the point above the meeting of the river San
Lorenzo and the sea. A marvelous meeting point — sea,
sun, sky, sound of the falling waves, the million intricate
white movements of the surf. Did I see God there —
whatever that is? There is harmony, everything fits one
with the other. So there is one?

Can it be thought of as a watchful agency? That I have
a problem with. Of course, there is the harmonization
of ourselves, our own organisms, with all the rest. This
gives it all quite a punch. My ears hear the bird singing
— are made to hear the bird singing. My nose smells

the fragrant plants. And it is beyond survival — these resonances. So it is like the million movements of the surf. The very complexity, the interweaving — that may be what Heschel calls the ineffable.

I shall have half a melon. My fast today will not exclude water, herb tea, juice and fruit.

Leaving Santa Cruz   Friday, October 6, 7:32 AM
What to say? On the road. The pick-you-up-at-home service instead of the Airporter. It is less of an adventure. With the Airporter I must carry my bags four or five blocks to Denny's at the mouth of the highway. There is darkness coming to light, and the Airporter is not there — will it be late? Then there are the other sleepy people. We are a community of travelers. Here, I am alone with the driver. He is tired, bored, listens to jack-a-rack music on the radio. I am alone, an individual, to be rocketed God knows where into a strange and silent universe.

And it is full light of another lovely Santa Cruz October day. We travel Highway 17, the mountain road. The treetops are gold — real gold — the gold of the all-powerful silent sun. I feel a wave of emotion. Pathos, fullness, as I write of the silent sun, golden morning. Why? I have been that way these days. Mr. Heschel puts me that way. What a desired state! It is awe of life — more than life, of existence. That there is a sun and trees and morning. Can one have a feeling like that after the first hours of daylight? Can I? I mean. Don't know.

The radio voice talks of OJ. Ai, Ai.   Thanks Bruce, then, it's Carl from San Francisco. The question being asked is: What would you say to OJ if you saw him on the street? So what has this to do with the gold treetops? It's maybe a free-floating anxiety, an itch, an irritation. Now the traffic has slowed to a stop. My nerves are grasping, reaching. Like a filament of white worm — reaching blindly for an attachment, a place to rest, to be able to move on from. Although I slept serenely last night. I knew I was alright as I slept. I was in my place and at rest. Surprising — I thought I'd be tossing in the night.

The radio voices rasp on my tranquility. Will it soon wear through? But no, it isn't tranquility — it is that sense of fullness mixed with that restless reaching of my nerve ends. I am on the edge. Edge of fatigue, probably. I am about to run out of steam — at eight in the morning. The rest of the day will be epilogue. Can I find a pool of quiet, a patch of velvet, a place within to curl into? Or will I be reaching nerves all the way to sleep in Portland, Maine? We will see.

8:06 AM   This is San Jose. The freeway. Cars everywhere. The radio commercials . . .

8:44 AM Gate C3. I feel semi-awful. Like a three-year-old too tired to relax. 9:30 in the morning may be too late to catch a plane — the full wave of fatigue has already arrived. Airport USA. Where do I ache? Well, I have a hollowed out feeling — seems to center around the roof of my mouth and go up to behind my eyes, and down my neck to a place to the front of my stomach and out my wrists. My legs seem okay. Sturdy old legs — you'll carry the rest of us forward. That's because the legs are not hollow. Unlike the rest of the body, the legs are filled with clunky chunky muscle. No brains. The brains don't go below the hips.

She just announced that all passengers to San Francisco

are boarding United Express at gate C3A. And no one came to the gate. They gave a flight and no one came. She calls again. Still no one. Here is a family — a one year old boy — his father carries him, and Ma with a two-year-old girl by the hand. Another young man sits on the floor with a little girl, looking out the window. Fathers with little kids, it's nice to see. There is a change. Maybe it will re-form America.   I'll read the *SF Chronicle*.

9:12 AM   Seat 25F — oddball in the corner pocket — about three feet from the engine. I must search for my earplugs. What kind of plane is this? Not a 737? — well, close — a B727 200. The family with the two kids is in the row in front of me. So far, I am the Lord of three seats, in the last row on this side. So in airplanemanship, it is okay — except for possible engine noise. I fish out my plastic baggie of earplugs. I have both red and white —always a choice. I choose white.   The Chinese proverb — the longest journey begins with a single step: I thought of that when I stumbled on the first step of the stairway to the plane door. But that wasn't the first step. The first step was over my own doorsill. That went fine, as I recollect.

9:41 AM   Poised, posed and purposeful. Now speeding.

9:42 AM   We have lift off, Mission Central. Below there is a land — autolandia — no, there are houses, too. And water. We turn before the water and head to the eastern hills. Whoops, we are doing an overturn. We are now heading south to Los Angeles.

Ah, she says we can call — I see — Airfone. Who can I call? Can I call God from Airfone? Hmm — I am still not clear on the concept. An un-verbalizable concept.

The brown hills wave under morning light. We are now heading for China. We are spiraling. Higher and higher — and we shall lift each other up.   Do I get lunch or breakfast on this? — oh my, the plane dipped down and I was very scared, looked about, tightened my seatbelt. When bump comes to jostle, I am not a believer in aerodynamics.

10:14 AM I missed the Sierras. I read through the Chronicle and when I looked out the window, Mono Lake was below, and the mountains behind.

2:50 PM (12:50 California time) Descending to Chicago. I napped wonderfully well for over an hour, lying across my three seats.   **2:59 PM** We are going through thick white fog. O'Hare is socked in. The plane joggles, toggles and quivers along. I read through the Hebrew alphabet over and over. Aleph, bet, gimmel, dalet . . .

3:09 PM The fog is thicker, the airplane slows down to 40 mph — who knows, there might be a semi-trailer stalled ahead. Ah, the ground appears, a dark, green-black place — ooh, green water. Is that Lake Michigan? Now we are again over the green-black land. A patch of emerald green, roads, houses, trees, lots of trees. Oh, looking up at the clouds, they are gray black. An angry sky over Chicago. It must be raining. Looks like California bungalows below. A small forest — gold and rust among the green. Autos: the main life form is now visible.

3:15 PM We have touchdown.

3:54 PM End of the line. Gate C29. O'Hare is a smickety smack airport. The concourses are roofed over like a 19th-century train station or the Crystal Palace. Lots of light. The fat man across from me is snoring, his arms folded over his briefcase. Out the glass wall I see cloud, gray on gray, not moving; yet I look up again and the gray on gray pattern has changed. Now I see bright blue patches up high.

I still feel hollowed out. Starts near the top of my head and comes down to my mouth, branches out either ear, then comes down to my stomach.   Four young people, 12 to 20, two boys, two girls, sit near me. All dressed in fresh new clothes — white or black canvas shoes, long shorts, the younger boy wears a large gold cross necklace over his dark green T-shirt. The older boy carries a large camcorder. They are excited, they are going someplace special. I think of my trip in 1951, with my parents, by train across the country and by ship to Europe and Israel. I carried a home movie camera. Somehow, it wasn't long ago. I feel that because, somehow, the essential has not changed. What I lacked then, I lack now. What I vaguely searched for then, I haven't yet found.

Outside, a drenching cloudburst, the water rolls down the tall windows. What was — am — I looking for? Meaning. What does it mean? How does one proceed? Isn't there more than desperately trying to meet expectations, doing this task or that to get by, to stay whole, to hang together, to be plausible, to act as if you know why you are doing it? Is there a ground of being, a ground of meaning, a ground floor? Didn't know, still don't. Is that a search for God? That seems to be the way Heschel talks. God is meaning, meaning is God.

Krishnamurti might put it another way. Life is its own meaning. But you must attend to life, see where life really is. No — existence rather than life. Or else grant that stones have life and the ocean and the sky are alive.

I smell pizza. Ah — the fat lady three seats down is eating pizza from a box. She looks satisfied, like a baby at the nipple. I have felt that way. That's life. I look at my watch — 2:21 PM (4:21 PM) — I have to remember it's still on California time.   So. Look for God? It's so presumptuous. I'd like you to meet my friend, God. Step right up folks and shake hands with God. First 3,000 will receive an all-expense-paid trip to Marine World. Next 10,000, a large pizza with salami. And cheese. Is God in O'Hare air terminal? We'll ask a panel of experts. Mr. Heschel. No, not Heschel, he's dead. So what, an expert has to be alive? Who else is on the panel?   I'm losing interest — the hollow space in my stomach has expanded.

5:12 PM   We have heightened security. As in "because of heightened security all the mailboxes in the airport have been sealed". So I shall keep until Portland the two postal cards I just wrote.

6:08 PM   Seat 26C. Another family in the row in front of me. Mother and father in their mid-40s, two boys about six and eight. I am hungry, but not tired. I have started on my second Heschel book, *God in Search of Man: A Philosophy of Judaism*. This one starts more clearly than *Man Is Not Alone*. I finished that one last night, just before I turned out the light. [**2017 note**: For more information on Abraham Joshua Heschel, a Jewish theologian and philosopher, see Page 219.]

8:30 PM (Maine time)   I have snacked. Miniscule

roast beef sandwich and hunk of cheese. I didn't eat the potato chips or the candy bar. The stewardesses are very busy — they seem to work harder serving these little box snacks than serving a full meal.

Portland, Maine, 11:31 PM   So to bed. David Becker picked me up at the airport. We talked and it became 11:30 — I would never stay up this late but it is still 8:30 in California.

On the island   Saturday, October 7, 12:57 PM
I say on the island because I'm not sure of the name — Mont Desert? We are approaching lunch. Amidst the flame of fall. Also mist and fog. Gray sea coves and windshield wipers. The road curves, rises, falls. The air is — can I say crisp? No, crisp implies dry. The air is moist, not quite raw. Am I in Maine? Mostly. Mostly Maine. Part still walking under the living October sun of Santa Cruz. There is a granite rock at the side of the road, sliced into slabs like Wonder Bread. My, what big knives you have, Grandmother Nature. We are going to Northeast Harbor. Or is it Northwest? Nor' by nor' west, through the squalls and the swells, o'er the crests and through the salt spray. Into the village, out of the village. Past the church.

∽ *2* ∾

Northeast Harbor

The world about us is astounding

Northeast Harbor   Sunday, October 8, 8 AM

Quiet magnificence. All is silent, all is sweet. The trees, as treely as can be, the great ocean, the gray sky, the yellow, orange and gold of fall amidst the dark evergreens. Me, on the third floor, looking past the neat windowpanes. And all silent, magnificently silent, silently magnificent. Marching in a grave and gracious procession through time. Fall, winter, up tide, down tide, new morning. One blackbird flies in front of the gray sky. My heart feels as calm and as full as the trees and the sea. I look at my watch — it is 8:07. Shall I go down to breakfast? A little fantasy goes through my mind. I go down. The only other person there is Weston's mother. We talk. She asks: And where are you from? And I tell her — my immigrant parents, my father made money in the junk business. My mind wanders to aunts and uncles. They were good people, I say to myself.

I look at the thick blue-green and white Chinese rug under me. I came in one generation from poor people, the unprivileged — actually the words that came to me were — "common people". I thought of the women serving last night. They are servers, servants. They are probably happy here. They associate with the quiet and comfort, the trees that stand stately and still, the quiet gray sea. When I was asleep last night, I was forming sleep speeches. One was the story of the ancient rabbi who said: When I come to God, he will not ask me Why were you not Moses; he will ask me Why were you not Zalma? I like that very much. I have absorbed it, I hope. I want very much to want to be Ralph, not to want to be X or Y or Z, who I have read of, who I meet. I want to fit within my own skin. Be a Jew, a gay man, be my own story, every bit, tatter, and triumph of it. Only then can I be part of the whole. The tree, the sea, all the suffering people.

1:43 PM   Elegance is mine, sayeth the Lord. The room is elegant, the chair comfortable, the lunch elegantly simple. I sit before the same bedroom window I sat before this morning. I feel nappy full — as in having eaten well and feeling like a nap. The sun may show this afternoon, for the solid gray of yesterday has changed to floating dark gray and bright white billows and beacons. I put on the blue canvas shoes I bought last year in Richelieu, France. Last year in Richelieu, this year in Northeast Harbor. My my. I look out the window. The trees haven't moved. And they won't. Trees are dependable. Strong silent types.

6:27 PM   I sit in the wicker chair in my bedroom, cooling after taking a very hot bath. It has been a pleasant day. In the morning, the eight of us sat in the room with the long sweet view down to the sea and talked of lives, questions, hopes, anxieties, class, money, gayness. A gracious lunch, then we drove to Jordan's Pond and walked two or three miles around it, past the gold, green, orange, scarlet trees. Then we drove the winding sea view roads of Acadia National Park on this Mount Desert Island, which seems to be the third largest island of the US coast — after Long Island and Martha's Vineyard.

Above: I point out Autumn in Maine; Below: Jordan's Pond

Northeast Harbor   Monday, October 9, 7:58 AM
There is a film of white mist over the windowpanes. Not
on the inside. Is it frost? No. There is another glass pane
outside the ones that slide up and down — what are they
called? The mist is on the outside of the inside panes.
So what? Well, lots of what: Beyond the sunlight is a
far shore and the still, blue sea. The world about us is
astounding in all its aspects. That is something I realize
once in a while. The silence of this place, the comfort, the
security, assists in that realization.

Before I went to the bathroom to wash up, I stood on the
aqua-light Chinese carpet and looked at the wicker chair
I am now sitting in. It stood on its legs on the carpet.
Quiet. I looked at the bed. It stood also. The lamp on the
dresser. They all stand, separate and still. They are in
a space and in a time. Steady and still and fragile and
disappearing. Here in a delicate way. More solid than
something only imagined — but of the same kind of stuff.
Imagined to a more solid state, but ephemeral things, as
is this house, as am I, the trees outside, the far shore,
the sea. Whose imagination created the trees? Is that an
anthropomorphic question? Just because imagination
created the bed, was imagination necessary for the tree?

I am at an interesting place in Heschel's book — the
second book, *God in Search of Man: A Philosophy of
Judaism.* He is talking of the difference between the
Greek and Jewish ways of looking at the world. He says
the Greek way is the foundation of philosophy. I haven't
gotten to his description of the Jewish way. Is there a
Jewish way of looking at the trees? I may be confusing
things with that question. Science is something else
again. I think.

So — I shall go down two flights of dark-wood stairs to the dining room. Breakfast, in comfort and security, with gentle morning light and wide green lawns, wide blue sea.

6:34 PM   After the hot bath, after the rock scramble walk. Peter, Jim and David left after lunch, so we are down to five.

10:25 PM   So to bed. After a walk the last hour. The five of us along the granite steps and gravel walks of a large public garden high above town lights and moonlit sea.

[**2017 note**: Starting in January 1994, eight gay men who had met through participation in a philanthropic organization called Threshold Foundation began meeting twice a year to discuss life and their lives. This gathering in Northeast Harbor was the fifth such meeting. Two of the men have since died and two have dropped out. Not all have come to every meeting, but in November 2017, three of us held the forty-ninth meeting in San Diego.]

∾ *3* ∾

Boston

"Still used by a free people"

Bangor, Maine airport   Tuesday, October 10, 12:51 PM

You are aware you are in an emergency exit seat? asks the stewardess.   I nod. Emergency Exit Expert Alpert — at your service. This is a real airplane, with propellers. We are going to Boston, sailing on sky clouds. We speed past the yellow flame trees and are up above gold green land. Above us the sky clouds. We approach the sky clouds slowly, flotillas of gray and white float overhead. Now we are in them, on them, with them.

At the beginning — I feel tired, a bit sweaty in the armpits, but I feel able to connect with the places in my head, inside my right knee, on either side of the bridge of my nose — the tired places. The deep shake of the engines wants to incorporate my head and heart. Nay, says my head, I shall move to a gentler rhythm. There is a man with a full head of white hair sitting three rows ahead. I am an admirer of old people with full heads of hair, now that I am not among them.

1:37 PM The voice from the ceiling says land ho —
Boston in ten minutes. I look out the window. A perfect
blue sea below, a fringe of low white clouds at the
horizon. A good day to be in Boston, a good day to be
alive. I am glad to be part of the sea blue planet. Land
ho — a dark green island in the white-blue sea. And,
directly ahead — it's North America!

This is Faneuil Hall . . . still used by a free people

Boston 4:52 PM Outside at a café alongside Faneuil
Hall. The brass plate at the corner of Faneuil Hall says
"still used by a free people". That gripped my heart.
Despite all the mishagas and injustice and horror, that
means something. When I visited the hall, there were
photos of Susan Anthony and Frederick Douglass. Those
are the kind of people, crazy for justice, who — what? —
move me, make it work.

A small dark leaf falls on this paper. I find that I think

a lot about the ongoing community. What happened 100, 200 years ago. I think of the men I met with this last weekend. I admire them greatly — their courage and honesty and confidence. I find it difficult to write now because I criticize myself every sentence. You are sentimental about Susan Anthony and Frederick Douglass, ignorant of who they were, what they did. Ai, Ai.

The weekend was a mixture. Feeling comfortable among people I admire and like much — even love, being cosseted in a great house in a magnificent site, hobnobbing with the very rich. And, at the same time, feeling the lack of social grace in me, not knowing the right spoon or the right phrase, not being easy in chat. Start from the most recent — the lunch with Robert at the airport. He is such an immensely accomplished person. Priest, lawyer, monk, congressional chief of staff, always pleasant and smiling. I admire him and like him, yet I don't know what to say to him. Likewise with Weston's mother — not really much older than me — perhaps ten years, but. But what? Great wealth, magnificent house, children and grandchildren, fluency and education and cultivated antecedents. Yet who is she to me? A mother. That daunting figure. Although she was very welcoming — and even, in all, quite vulnerable. A person among people, facing the difficulties of living, facing death.

But as these dear friends talk of the high ones, the renowned and very rich ones, the proper and accepted ones, I was dumb. Not that I felt badly. It is quite interesting. It was not that I was in this great house, but that I was in someone else's house. I am surprised at myself — that I have carried myself as well as I have.

I am where I do not expect — have not expected — to be. I never was to be rich, or sitting with the highborn. Yet, I know that great wealth and birth into great wealth are incidents — like hair color and foot size. If one has enough to live in a decent manner, more money   — oh my — police cars, two ambulances with shrill horns and flashing lights — a great clamor. What is going on?

So — what was I saying? Great wealth — over adequate wealth — doesn't much change the issues and parameters of life. If you think so, it is only because you are outside, looking in, with inadequate knowledge. There is the same inner hurt in meeting others, the same inadequacy of meanings, the same driving urges and ego, the same sickness and fear of death. All the real things, the important things, are the same.

Now it is 5:33 — the sunlight has disappeared, except from the upper stories of a tall building a few blocks off to my left and the blazing windows of the building behind me. Before the light goes, I'll walk about central Boston.

6:38 PM   In the bus which goes from the subway station to the airport terminal building. It is now quite dark.

8:14 PM   Boston airport, gate 19. They have started boarding the plane. I doubt that I'll write much during this flight. It will be a long night — no, a short night — to Paris. And then almost as long for Paris to Tel Aviv.

8:36 PM   On the plane, seat 26-4. Oh my — how I am. I watch the other people come down the aisle, struggle with bags. I worry about my canvas hat, which I have put in the overhead bin — will someone put some things on top of it and crush it? A big muscular man carries a large duffel bag to the row in front of me and tries to stuff it in an overhead bin. Too big, it won't go in. I feel smug. A little victorious? I bother myself — I am so petty, so hostile, competitive over something. Living space? I don't want to be that way. Of course, it is late, I am tired. But I fear I have a nasty streak. I separate from other people.

10 PM   Peanuts and grapefruit juice. I have nothing to say, but I want to write. I feel faintly fatigued even now.

Paris   Wednesday, October 11, 9:43 AM (4:43 AM in Boston)
Sitting in a glassed-in security lounge, waiting to re-board the airplane. Very tired. Paris is caught in deep white fog.

~ *4* ⌇

Israel: Netanya

Fat dates and the blood-warm Mediterranean

About to land in Israel   Still Wednesday, 4:11 PM
Just a thought — what I wish for myself here: to be open
to those I meet, to appreciate them. I thought of Rita —
to be Rita-esque. Though, more feasible — to be me-esque
and aware of how I relate to people.

5:07 PM   On the highway five minutes out of Ben-
Gurion Airport. So here I am — writing instead of
making friends with the driver. An elephant has a long
nose — what are you going to do about it? Also, I write
because the sun is an orange ball just disappearing
and I won't be able to write later. Besides, the driver
is listening to chatter in Hebrew over the intercom.
We are on a six-lane highway. Could be just outside
of Watsonville, except the green road sign says Haifa.
And the big blue truck alongside has legends in yellow
Hebrew letters printed on its sides. A flat brown land. In
the distance, white apartment blocks. The driver is going
too fast. The first thing I asked him was: How long does it
take to get to Netanya? I don't know, he said, it depends
on . . . — and he never finished the sentence. Maybe the

finish is: how close to death's door we drive. Now we are in a city and the roadway is eight lanes.

My — glass high-rises. Only the Hebrew signs distinguish it from California. I have seen Tel Aviv change over the decades. When I first saw it in 1951 it was a simple and pleasant sea-side city in the sand dunes. Look, says the driver as we slow to ten mph — he waves at the cars about us. Because of this, he says, I don't know how much time. This is the busy hour? I say. All the time, he says. We cross a small river. The Yarkon? We seem to have passed the center of the city. Here there are many trees. I am recognizing some of the Hebrew words in the intercom chatter. Shlosha — I think that is three? And the fellow says Toda raba, which means Thanks a lot — I think. The green road signs are in both Hebrew and Roman characters. We seem to be out of Tel Aviv now, but the roadway is still eight lanes. Here we come to a divide — one way to Haifa/Hertzlia, the other Raana —something like that. A stoplight — this is the end of the expressway, I guess. We pass an intercity — or tourist —bus. On the side, it says "air-conditioned, video". I think we are on the coastal road now — Hasira Interchange, says a green sign. There's a sign — Hertzlia, with an arrow directing off. It is getting too dark to write.

Netanya 5:57 PM   Hurrah! Journey's end: room 211, Green Beach Hotel, Netanya. A simple room, a student's room, albeit without a desk. And the timing? Parfait. Supper is at 7 PM — so I have time to unpack and take a shower. And I am excited about studying. For it is my metier — studying.

7:47 PM   No question. I love this place. Supper was

in a Sukkot hut made of palm branches and cloth. A wonderful buffet — hummus, tomatoes, herring, yogurt — all that kind of stuff. At my table were an American woman from Florida, a woman from Paris who has a second home in Caesarea, a young man from Paris, and a Japanese woman. I spoke French to the French woman, who doesn't know English. The setting is Graham Greene. Graham Greene? — some English novelist. The warm air, the near sea, the mix of people. Now there is something happening at eight — maybe singing.

Netanya   Thursday, October 12, 1:51 AM
I was reluctant to turn on the light because I want to sleep through to morning my first night in Israel. But I was awake; it was not easy to find the place in my head where I was and follow it down to sleep. I think this is partly because the place where I was, was washed over by the sound. The sound is not a loud sound. It could almost be the wind in the trees or the sea along the shore. Last night I thought it might be the sea. But no, it resonates with the vibration left in my body by the cutting jet engines. It is the sound of the Tel Aviv to Haifa Expressway — the rush of metal cutting the air. I hear it also in my bedroom at home when I open the window to the garden. There was no sound like it at the great house in Northeast Harbor, Mount Desert Island, Maine. That is one reason I slept so well there. The other was the long walks we took every day. Another, more elusive and less tangible reason was that my ego was swaddled in money, my body in every comfort and a calmly delightful natural sensorium.

Oh, I have so much to talk about now. I could write until morning had I the physical and nervous energy. I woke dreaming of Hitler and the Holocaust. Of Hitler's son, of the document that somehow resolved the terrible conundrum of why it happened. Without that resolution there would be no way to continue living. I also thought before I was fully awake, that I have put myself in play on this trip. The concept of Ralph Alpert. Jew, rich man, gay man. Jews, parents, America, Christians, Hitler and Holocaust. Oh my, much more. Body and soul, prick and gray mind jelly. I shall see if I can go back to sleep, for it is 2:12 AM.

6:11 AM   I wake feeling I could sleep on for several hours. But this is my first day and I have much to do. My dreams, ever since I left home last Friday, have been powerful. As I woke now I was dreaming a dream of fighters for social justice. I can't remember details, but at the end a civil liberties lawyer was describing how Fidel Castro worked as an actor in San Francisco. He was not an actor like you, he said, but in his own way he was very good.

7:44 AM   After my Israeli breakfast of cheese, tomatoes, bell pepper, cucumber, bread and tea. There is the blue sea, the sand dunes, rough green lawns, low white buildings — all the lovely Mediterranean artifacts. I'm so happy I came here first instead of going immediately to Jerusalem. It feels like the right place at the right time. I shall study my aleph bet a bit before class begins.

11:30 AM   I am listening to a lecture by a scribe — he who writes the Torah. He says the scribes must bring holiness to each letter of the 300,000 some. He speaks English, then a woman translates to Russian, for there are many Russians here.

2:26 PM   Riding around in a tour bus with all the

students. Milk and honey seep from the ground. Pecans and pomegranates, olives and bananas and mangoes. Red tile roofs. We go slowly — through a moshav (rural collective). We are just a couple miles from Netanya. A golden bunch of fat dates hangs from a palm tree. When they said honey in the Bible, says our teacher with a microphone, this is what they meant. Now we come to an open field — a mile away are the tall buildings of Netanya. We pass a large grove of small orange trees. But a quarter mile along, the trees are cleared away. Highrise apartment buildings seem to be today's crop. Now we pass through an industrial area. I see "Microsoft" in Roman letters on a sign on a building. I remember how, in 1951, I was surprised to find toothpaste made in Israel. More apartment buildings being built. Developer's signs — "Sea View". Oh, we are beside the sea.

3:21 PM   Now we are all in the Yemenite Museum of the city of Netanya. The curator talks in Hebrew, a teacher translates to English and the assistant curator to Russian. It proceeds slowly. We started 3500 years ago. Tribes. David, Solomon, the temple. It's much more impressive in Hebrew: Shlomo Ha-melech, so on. Cohens, the Levis and the others. Ha Assur — the Assyrians? — destroy the whole country except for the tribes of Benjamin and Judah. The ten lost tribes. Nebuchadnezzar. The exiles. And Israelites went to Yemen about 2500 years ago. Almost no Jews left in Israel. Persians said you can return — at that time Israelites had been in Yemen only 70 years. But Jews in Yemen refused to come back because they had received a prophecy that the temple would be destroyed again. They would not come back until the Messiah came. And after 500 years the Romans destroyed the temple again.

So that is why Yemenites are so close to the teachings of ancient times. Yemen was far from the center of events in the Mid-East. When Islam came, Yemen was fiercely fundamentalist. And it was necessary to be very Muslim or very Jewish. So when the Yemenites came to Israel 50 years ago, they came like the biblical tribes. There you have it all in a shattered nutshell. Now we are going to look at a movie.

4:45 PM   I walk about the museum. There is a picture of a group of Yemenites on an airplane in the 1950s. An old woman's face touches my heart.

The Mediterranean at Netanya

5:02 PM   I sit on a bench at the edge of a cliff. Below is the beach and the sea. It is already twilight. I am suddenly very tired. When the group came down the four flights of stairs from the Yemenite museum, I went down a different stairway from most of the other people. Then I stopped in a shop to buy a postcard. Now I have turned 65 and all the others are gone and it is sunset beyond the Mediterranean. A fat woman in a pink dress calls in French to someone. A small child cries Aabaa, Aabaa — looking for a father. The bus will leave the Central Square at 6:30. What to do until 6:30? Until 80? First, I shall go to a café and order an orange juice.

5:19 PM   The restaurant Tahiti — I sit at an outside table. It will soon be quite dark. A motor scooter buzzes by.

Netanya   Saturday, October 14, 8:32 PM
Back in room 211, the Green Beach Hotel — Hofa Arack. With a headache. My cousin and her husband came here yesterday afternoon. We went to the Tel Aviv hospital in which lies my cousin's mother (who is also my cousin). Wrecked, wracked by age and sickness. Wasted to angular bones and discolored skin, coughing uselessly to clear her lungs, a hole in her throat for a tube, unable to talk. A nightmare. But, my cousin says, she is much improved from last week, when a breathing tube and intravenous feeding tube were attached to her. After 7:30 we came to my cousin's apartment in Rishon LeZion. Today I was the whole day in the apartment, talking with the three grown children and assorted other family, and eating a large dinner. And listening to much Hebrew being spoken. Which I think is helpful to my learning.

So. Let's see if I can write the alphabet.

ל   כ   י   ט   ח   ז   ו   ה   ד   ג   ב   א
ת   ש   ר   ק   צ   פ   ע   ס   נ   מ

I had to look at a paper to do it.   Alef Bet Gimmel Dalet Hay Vav Zayin Chat Tet Yod Kaf Lamed Mem Nun Samech Ayen Pey Tsade Qof Resh Shin Tav.   How much of our culture is drift and chance! We have the Roman alphabet, our days are named after Norse gods. What is there that is not chance, that is meant to be?

My cousin Zhava (second from left) with some family, and me

Netanya   Sunday, October 15, 2:40 PM
I sit on the edge of my bed in room 211. I wait for yet another cousin. This would be a third cousin, I think, for he is two generations beyond me. He was scheduled to arrive at 2:30. Until a few minutes ago I was napping. But not napping. It is something of a finding exercise. I lie down, put a handkerchief over my eyes, and I follow something somewhere. A sense, a sensation, usually in my head, and I follow down or deep. Something like Alice in Wonderland. What do I discover? Not sure. I probably am sleeping.

I had this thought this morning in class: From seeing my cousin, wasted and wracked, in the hospital. She, like my mother, had what I think of as a rabbity disposition. Or a bird — my mother's name, in fact, was Bird: Feigel, Feigele. Though, in America she was called Fannie. What I mean by rabbity disposition is that condition of always being on the alert. Lest the cat jump and catch you unaware, not ready to fly. A nervous energy, wary fidget, constant activity. A tiring kind of disposition — that is what I think. And my mother died relatively young — at 72. Fruma, my cousin, is almost 80. But she looks as if the vital force has all escaped, been used up.

So. I admonished myself: You — you too — may fidget it all away in useless wariness, in subterranean fidget and fuss. I thought of it as I sat in class and I felt the fidget quiet down a bit. So I won't learn, so I won't shine, so I won't be esteemed, so I will be in danger. The danger is unavoidable. Be in it, and don't fidget. March on, into the fire and until the last ember. But calmly, knowing what I know, of the river and the fire and the ceaseless generation. Be in it, flow with it, burn with it.

The other event of this morning was that at the 10:30 break I walked to the sea — the blood-warm Mediterranean. I crossed the white sand and dipped my hand in the wine-dark sea (actually, it is a happy sea-blue). This is the sea of Moses and the army of Agamemnon. No — Moses never crossed over the Jordan. Maybe he saw the Mediterranean as a boy in Egypt. Mitzraim. Hebrew has different names for countries. I ran across the name of France yesterday. What was it? I'll look it up in my dictionary now. No — not there — no proper nouns. It starts with an S.

∽ *5* ∼

Rishon LeZion

An illiterate observer of prayer

Rishon LeZion Still Sunday, 4:51 PM

Rishon LeZion

Now I am at my other cousin's. We drove the expressway from Netanya. Israel seems very much of the West — it appears a modern, first-world country, with its expressways and white buildings, built or being built. I remember when I first came here, in 1951, I saw Israel as a place very different from Europe — which I had just seen for the first time. Europe was green, luxuriantly green, Israel was brown dry. And it seemed to lack the green of money — there was a stringency about it, centuries of dry struggle.

Rishon Le Zion   Monday, October 16, 6:34 AM
Outside, beyond the window, bright buildings and bright
sky. I sit on the cot I slept on last night. I shall go to
synagogue again with the men this morning. Because
these cousins are observant Orthodox, because today
is Simcha Torah, the celebration of starting the yearly
cycle of reading the Torah. I say again because I went
last night. Two hours of dancing and singing in the
synagogue.

7:13 AM   The first one up, I sit on the white leatherette
couch in the living room. But no — the first one up was
the little white poodle and it dances about me. Just
outside the window are bright flowers — jacaranda? It
is the Mediterranean — south of France, Italy, Greece
— the flowers, the doves cooing somewhere, the bright
morning sunlight, the white buildings. Why doesn't
Santa Cruz have this Mediterranean flavor? Well, there
is the fog that comes off the Pacific. And the Victorian
houses — which are not houses adapted to a warm, sun-
drenched place. But Santa Cruz is not sun-drenched.
Drenched — a striking word. Drenched donuts. Drenched
survivors of a ship wreck. Rain-drenched, sun-drenched.
It must come from old Norse. The old Norse knew
drenching.

I am not sure I am doing the right thing. The right
thing, in my fevered imagination — the right thing
in this house on a holy day is no work. And who knows
what is work and what is not. Yesterday evening on our
way to and from Shul, we walked down and then up the
five flights of stairs instead of taking the elevator. Now
— is taking an elevator work? Apparently — it may be
the pushing of the button. But whatever the minuteness

it may become — I am in favor. It seems to me that not using the elevator is a fine and noble thing. It takes us from crazed mechanisms to our own feet. That is a sane thing to do on occasion. Come to earth, be self-reliant, live in a simpler world. Know that it exists, can be re-created, that we can come back to it. Now — how about scribbling? For me it is not counted as work. Except on the farm in Spain, where one has to appear to be working much of the time. And, occasionally in a café, when one wants to be taken as writing incredibly insightful essays or fiction truer than reality.

So — now it is past 7:30 and I hear no sound from the six other people in this apartment. From somewhere outside I hear, faintly, singing — ancient chants or American rock? Sounds more like the chants. I look at the floor — tan and white terrazzo squares — the same as Pepin's apartment in Madrid. Suddenly, I am tired of America, of wall-to-wall carpet, of brawny expansiveness, of unrelenting movement. Not that this is serene. Just not as rich, making-do more. Maybe, also, there is less contrast between rich and poor here. This is not something I have seen yet; I imagine it. But one facet of America that wearies Americans much more than they realize is the poor. To see beggars and aimless people in the streets. They are not random and freakish appearances. They make manifest something that is shot through all of American society. Aimlessness, hopelessness. Yes? No? Much of the television over here is American crap. The great unreality of wealth, leisure, physical beauty and health.   Ah, others are awake and about.

5:55 PM   Rishon LeZion   So. I sit on the white couch, a holiday having passed since last I wrote. For now, darkness is on the land and Simcha Torah is over. I went to synagogue at 8 AM this morning with my cousin's husband, whose name is, to the best of my knowledge, Meyer. A very nice fellow. I was an illiterate observer through an hour and a half of prayer. Then the dancing and singing began and lasted for the next two hours. They really jumped and jammed. Lots of energy, enthusiasm and genuine joy. The synagogue is about three blocks from this apartment. It is part of a religious grade school. There's no rabbi. There were some 100 or 150 men who mostly wore white shirts, dark pants, the small knitted skullcap and the white prayer shawl with black stripes. There were also many boys — from toddlers to teenagers. The synagogue is a simple and simply furnished room with seats on three sides and the ark of the covenant at the fourth side. There is a sort of movable platform with a lectern in the middle. The men were people of the neighborhood, middle-class people. Women? Yes. I didn't see them until I had been there a while last night. They sit in the back of the bus, behind the lace curtain. This was the only element of it all that I found uncongenial.

6:09 PM   Now people are stirring. After we came back from the service about 1 PM, we had a large dinner. Then tea — and throughout I listened to the others talk. Which I tend to do even when I know the language. And now — the listening helps me learn. I hear words I already know — I ask about some words I hear.

32

~ *6* ~
The Green Beach Hotel

An island of learning in a sea of tumult

Netanya   Wednesday, October 18, 6:03 AM
Just a few words to begin the day. As if the wonder of birds had not already done so. The birds squeak, tweak, squangle outside and the light has arrived — בקר שמונה — the eighth morning.   So, I shall quickly dress and walk by the sea before breakfast.

[2017 note: With respect to Hebrew words and phrases, keep in mind that Hebrew is read in the opposite direction from English: that is, from right to left.]

Netanya   Thursday, October 19, 2:35 PM
Full sun, as I sit on the curb beside the bus stop for the Number 7 bus. This is right across the road from the entrance to החוף הירק — otherwise called the Green Beach Hotel. Which is where Ulpan Akiva, my school, is located.

2:42 PM   I move across the road, close by the outer wall of the hotel, where there is shade. There are, on this, the shady side of the road, some ten kids speaking animatedly in Russian and five or six adults — all waiting for the bus, I assume. Across the road, in the sun at the bus stop, stands only one — a stout man in white shirt, black trousers, black hat and white beard. Ah, now a car stops and he gets in. How come no one offered me a ride when I sat in the sun? Sometimes, I think of the automobile as a nifty invention. When I have one at beck and call however, I usually think of autos, in the mass, as damnable nuisances. Bus Number 7 goes to the central bus station in Netanya — it takes a half hour because it winds about through several different neighborhoods.

2:54 PM On the bus, down the beachside road, turn, and in the distance I see the white apartment blocks of Netanya.

4:55 PM Once again on Number 7, at the central bus station. Sitting in the back of the bus. I have been on a semi-silent journey in the center. I walked to an indoor shopping mall first. There's something about this city — about Israel — that strikes me. It is and it is not like America and Western Europe. The "is like" strikes me first: expressways, autos (mostly Japanese), square white buildings with square windows, modern buses. The "is not" part is vaguer. Something caught by time. The shops that, even in the new mall, are small, crowded, inward. Maybe it is something in me. Boyle Heights, Los Angeles — Jewish shops in the 1930s. The cornucopia doesn't quite tip, it doesn't flow. Yet, now we come to the boulevard by the sea and to a tall modern apartment house or hotel right on the beach. And three or four floating parasails. That's not 1938 Boyle Heights.

I spoke at breakfast with a young fellow who is in my

class — Jonah — he comes from Santa Fe, is in college in the US, studying philosophy. A serious guy. He is at this school for five months so he will learn Hebrew well. I don't think I will move here, he said. Though several of his family live in Israel. Maybe he feels what I feel now — there is something crabbed, tight, here. Does it come from Eastern Europe — the bureaucracy? Come from the Middle East — harshness, poverty? All that has mixed with America and 3000 years of Jewish life and teaching.

5:15 PM   It is becoming too dark to write.

Netanya, the Green Beach Hotel   Friday, October 20, 3:26 PM

Sitting on the terrace, a frisky breeze and a balmy sun. A little tan and black puppy sleeps in the sun a few feet away. He is so alive in his sleep, so well placed, perfectly at home in the world. He is doing what is done, what is well done. He is one with the sun, the sea, the air. He is a fat little puppy. I catch a little of his place. I too am in the sun, in the sea breeze, with the sound of the sea, the birds, the ruffling pages, the long green banana leaves, the fat white and gray clouds easily moving overhead.

Netanya   Monday, October 23, 8:08 PM

My, I haven't written in this since Friday. Now I lie on my bed in room 211 — there being no chair in the room. I just walked out the door to go to the choir, then came back to get my long-sight glasses. And then decided to write instead of going to the singing. The last week has passed as a pattern of class and then afternoon study. Almost every morning I go out before 6:30 and walk down to the sea and walk a ways on the wet sand near the water. It is a raffish dirty-ish shore. Bits of plastic, truck tracks across the sand, the acrid smell of something burning. Just a few people about — mostly early morning exercisers. On Saturday morning, even though I was on the beach not long after 5:30, there were several men fishing into the surf. Three young fellows were out in the surf with a net, others had lines cast out. This morning I walked the other way — south of the hotel — and came on a stable with some dozen horses. I assume they rent horses.

The hotel is completely surrounded by a concrete wall six or eight feet high. I'm not sure why — but I have a dim memory of a story of terrorists coming in around here by boat some years back. On Saturday morning when I came to the gate at 5:30, it was fastened shut with chain and lock. I heard someone yelling at me from the terrace of the hotel in Hebrew. Ani lo yoded Ivrit, I yelled back, proud of myself for doing a whole Hebrew sentence. He pointed and I saw there was a guardhouse near the gate. I rapped on the door and a fellow came out and opened the gate for me.

So — after my daily morning walk I wash up and go to breakfast at the hotel. The dining room (and bar, reception desk, etc.) is in a two-story building near the gate. The rooms are in a dozen other buildings scattered out on the grounds. The school is a group of one-story classrooms and offices set off to one corner of the compound. Breakfast is a buffet: big bowls of cottage cheese, a sort of creme fraiche, feta cheese, slices of Swiss cheese, sliced tomatoes, chunks of cucumber, olives, slices of red and green pepper, yogurt, eggs (both scrambled and hard-boiled), and some very sweet corn flakes. It is easy to eat too much. Oh, I forgot the herring — three kinds of pickled herring.

Rooms at the Green Beach Hotel

Class begins at 8 AM. I am in Kitah (class) Aleph — the beginning of the beginning. It is large for a language class — about 20. About half Russian immigrants, who seem to speak only Russian, three French speakers — a middle-aged woman who owns the best-known Jewish restaurant in Paris, a young fellow, who may be a lawyer, from Toulon, and a young woman. There are only two Americans besides me — a woman from Florida (a devout Catholic) and a college-age fellow from Santa Fe. The rest: a very bright 18-year-old girl from Vienna, a woman psychologist from Argentina (who is immigrating here with her three teenage kids), a woman from Norway, two young Arab women, one from Nablus. There was a young woman from Cape Town, South Africa, but she hasn't shown up for the last several days. The variety of people at this school is astonishing. There are at least three Japanese, a man from Singapore, many Arabs. There is a 93-year-old Englishman who was a hero in the 1948 War of Independence and seems to still hold a high honorary rank in the Israeli army.

There is the loudspeaker. One of the less pleasant features of the place is that the only phones for guests are in the main building and when a call comes in for someone, they call for the person over a very loud speaker. The other sound I hear is an airplane. There are airplanes overhead a lot. A helicopter flies along the shore every hour or so. And light planes go by frequently. Yesterday there was a flyby of squadrons of jet fighters from the Israeli and Jordanian air forces. They overflew all of both countries in something like an hour. It was to commemorate the first anniversary of the signing of a peace agreement between the two countries.

So — classes go until 1 PM, with breaks at 9:30 (ten minutes), 10:30 (half hour), and 12 (ten minutes). Sometimes, from 12 to 1 there is a talk or singing instead of the regular class. At 1, there is lunch, which is the big meal.

A view of the Green Beach Hotel and Ulpan Akiva

I will read a while now — in Heschel's *God in Search of Man: A Philosophy of Judaism*. I am now at page 93, of a total of 426. Heschel catches me and loses me. Right now, I am asking: Is there a male sub-text to Judaism? The language is very gendered. Heschel says things like:

> "to the Greeks, as to many other peoples, the earth is generally known as Mother Earth. She is the mother who sends up fruits, the giver of children . . . The adoration of the beauty and abundance of the earth in Greek literature is tinged with a sense of gratefulness to the earth for her gifts to man. Such a concept is alien to Biblical man. He recognizes only one parent: God as his father . . . The prophets and the psalmists do not honor or exalt the earth, though dwelling on her grandeur and abundance. They utter praise to Him who created her."

Having read Riane Eisler, this language sends up flags, bells and whistles. He who gave birth to her — what is this all about?

Netanya   Tuesday, October 24, 4:47 PM
The sun has set; dusk comes upon the land. Israel has time just one hour behind Western Europe. So — it gets light very early and dark very early. Even with God on your side, the sun sets by sun time.

I sit in Room 211, window and door open, outside the birds twitter and there is the noise of the tractor lawnmower — going right by the window now. A warm wind pours through the door and out the window. I have done most of my homework. What to do now? Earlier I had an idea to take Number 7 bus to town, go to the bank, the post office. I walked to the bus stop, changed my mind. I have no time for bus rides. Birds, beach, walk, read. These are much more important.

Netanya   Wednesday, October 25, 10:47 AM
I sit, only but not lonely, in classroom 12. Where there is to be the talk in Sephardit (French). About Jerusalem, where we go tomorrow. On a bus, leaving at 5:30 AM. By sitting in this room I do a double — learning French as I learn Hebrew. I did the same yesterday morning when there were lectures on the political situation in the Middle East. I understood most of it and was very interested. But could I repeat or summarize the French lecture? It would be difficult.

So. Here I am — on an island of learning in a sea of tumult. I like it, I cotton to the rhythm: the early morning walk by the sea, breakfast, class, lunch, study, lecture, sleep. No place to go, nothing to do but study. With my own room — a haven, a safe harbor. I see that at the side of this classroom there is a bathroom door. I didn't know that until yesterday when I came into room 12 for the first time. My class meets next door, in room 11.   Ah — here enter a group of French speakers.   As to the bathroom, it is typical of me that I wouldn't know there is a bathroom next door — I have been walking the hundred meters to my room to pee. I am not one who quickly clues in. An endangered species type: safe on the island, but gets wet in the sea, swallows saltwater, flops and flounders.   My — the noise level here is astounding — a babble, rumble and rattle of French. No orderly Anglos here.

40

7

Jerusalem Visit

Arriving two years after King David

Netanya   Thursday, October 26, 5:11 AM
Early. And earlier I rose. I woke at — what? 2:30? 3:45?
I got out of bed about an hour ago. Why? At 5:30 the bus
leaves for Jerusalem. With all the school upon it.

5:37 AM   In the second row of an elegant tour bus. In
the first row rides the shotgun. Like the Old West. The
man with a rifle sits behind the driver. Now there is
confusion — a coming and going — for the announcement
has been made that this bus is English, French and
Arabic. The second bus, that just pulled up outside the
gate, is for Russian and Hebrew. And the light comes
over the sky: pink-rose haze and pale gray-blue. The
submachine gun just came aboard. So we shall have
a rifle and a submachine gun. Already I am nervous.
Where is John Wayne (the airport)? This is a novel in
the making. From the sea to Jerusalem, pink and blue,
Russian, Arabic and French. Oh, Oh. The submachine
gun is going to the Russian bus. We have only the rifle.

5:52 AM   We have movement. The bus rolls out the gate

— into the unsheltered outer world. Across the coastal hills we shall go, tunnel into time.   There are the sand dunes, a quiet gray Mediterranean, the unfinished new apartments.   The bus stops. Why? Another student gets on — he has been running. He almost missed the bus-through-time.   More apartments being built. Morning traffic gathers around us. Past the pecan trees, then a mess of industrial buildings. The sun will also rise. God's sun, from out of Jerusalem. Past the orange trees. Now the sun, which shines through the haze like a gold-yellow full moon, over the gray cypress screen.   A stoplight — we turn the wrong way — toward the sea — maybe we are driving to Athens. Goodbye Solomon, hello Socrates.

Now the sun is on high beam, drilling in from dead left. Gray buildings with metal apparatus, plowed brown fields, gasoline station at a crossroads, high-power transmission line. Rickety rack — here come apartment buildings. Little gray and brown cars with sharp red tail lights pile up in front of us. The electric lines are overhead again. From the sun — I mean, the sun says we are going south. To Egypt, Mitzraim. Who would we listen to in Egypt? Who would tell us the wisdom of Egypt? What is the wisdom of Egypt? How could I reach 65 knowing almost nothing? Big blue road sign overhead. Jerusalem, it says.   We stop at a light. In front is the crossing of a super-duper highway. The sun has blazed higher, into overpowering presence.

The man with the mike, Ozzie, is a teacher at the Ulpan. One sentence in English, another in Hebrew. The land of milk and money, he says.   Passing Bar-Ilan University. We are on the freeway, the buildings rise and pass. We will soon turn to the right, pass Ben-Gurion Airport, he says.   We pass a great flat-topped mound. The garbage of Tel Aviv, he says. Now he reads a prayer for the road: that we return safely. Baruch ata adonai . . . Amen, say the voices at the end. Now the sun has swung to the left front. The fellow across the aisle, the lawyer with the southern accent, begins to tell Ozzie, the teacher, about Jewish Renewal and Rabbi Zalmon Schachter. **[2017 note:** For more on Zalmon Schachter, see Page 220.] We are passing Ben-Gurion Airport. The road turns, we head directly into the sun.

A line of hills comes forth from the mist of the East. Like the first hills as you head east from Sacramento toward the Sierra Nevada. We begin to climb, we are ascending — to Jerusalem. Four lanes divided. A tour bus ahead of us, a tour bus to the left of us. Pale brown fields, an electric transmission line to the right. The city is behind us, we are going across the land. It is now almost a quarter to 7. The world is hazed over. Is it the tinted bus windows, or is it the Hamsin, the wind from the desert with dust to air, or is it just plain smog? Dark brown plowed fields, hills and shapes of hills before us. Latrun monastery — from crusader times; a blue and white Israeli flag. A memorial place, Ozzie says. Twenty-five kilometers yet to Jerusalem. We will stop at Abu Gosh, an Arab village. We pass a eucalyptus forest. A plaintive, quiet, song in front — the driver's music. An orchard — figs? An Arab man, black coat, head covering, walks along the side of the expressway. Burned trees — there was a fire here several weeks ago, Ozzie says. There, by road side, the rusted remains of the trucks of 1948. The phone rings. What? Yes. The driver answers. A call for Ophir, our leader. He talks, the driver's music rises. Higher and higher we go. Slowly, behind the little autos. Ah, we turn off the highway — we are going to eat breakfast.

[**A 2017 memory:** Breakfast on the early morning ride to Jerusalem was picnic style, at a roadside open space. I ate sitting with a young Palestinian doctor, who was a student of Hebrew at the Ulpan (school), a pleasant and serious fellow. He worked in a refugee camp in Gaza and talked of the poverty and misery of the camps.]

Elvis statue at Elvis Inn

7:30 AM   Elvis Inn. With an eight-foot statue and Coca-Cola billboards. I lean against a fence. A fresh wind catches this paper. A camel, says the southern lawyer: down the hill, beyond the sickly trees, before the blue water tank.

7:58 AM   There is the mist, the hills come in dark shapes, the earth alongside the road is tawny and grey, looks wrung out dry. Here is a small grove of dark green trees. Pines? Ein Karem, Hadassah Hospital, monastery.

3:59 PM   Tired. As I left the Old City through the gate by the Western Wall, King David was being interviewed. He wore a long blue gown and a golden skullcap. The interviewer, a middle-aged woman in dark blue, was videotaping it. How long have you been in Jerusalem, King David? Two years. Before that? Australia. His whole family — two kids — is here with him.

⌁ *8* ⌁

Rishon LeZion Again

Maybe God is a ugaboo too

Rishon LeZion   **Saturday, October 28, 6:57 AM**
Morning. Sitting on my bed in this dim room. Automobiles, birds. I feel my back bowed as I sit and write. I feel calm, mostly rested yet not rested — I have never been rested, at rest. Alert, yet not alert. The not-rested is the not-alert. Many thoughts, memories, suppositions, insights. Two weeks and two days of studying Hebrew. Phrases and words in my mouth.

I think of being in Jerusalem the next two weeks. I have talked with the fellow I may study with in Jerusalem — study Judaism, whatever that is. Reading Heschel's book, what strikes me is the correspondence between the way this Jewish philosopher sees the world and the way Krishnamurti, coming from Indian tradition, sees the world. Something about the way of apprehending reality. It is not through thought. There is an immediate intuitive grasp. Heschel talks about awe, the ineffable. Krishnamurti talks of perceiving without the screen of the past, the conceptual structure that takes the life out of reality by reducing it to categories and concepts. So —

I don't know why the mishmash of me should be closer to reality now than previously. I have less sense — ability to sense — and less energy than before. But — anyway the learning interests me. The possibility excites me. So to rise — at the favorable hour of 7:11. [**2017 note**: For a brief note on Krishnamurti, see page 223.]

7:49 AM   I sit on the chair, washed, shaved, toothbrushed. And snuffle and scritch and scratch. Ears, nose. Outside, a cat meows, people speak in another apartment. Did I say where I am? I am in the apartment of my relatives in Rishon LeZion. Third floor. I am in the bedroom of Dror, one of the boys, who went to stay at his married sister's house — to make room for me, I think. The day, the morning, seems heavy. Heavy gray-white sky, heavy humid air. Yesterday, just before dawn, it rained for the first time of the season. A shower. The change of weather started Wednesday with the Hamsin, the hot wind from the desert. On Thursday, in Jerusalem, the heat continued but by evening dark clouds covered the sky. I now recognize in Hamsin the word "ham" (hot).

I take off my glasses, rub my face. I miss my early morning walk by the sea (ha yam). The day sits heavy and waits. Although the birds sing. There are many birds in Israel. They sing a whirl of noise out of the trees at the Green Beach Hotel in the morning. But I saw no sea birds — no gulls or sandpipers along the surf — only an occasional big black raven on the dry sand. Why is that?

Now I hear the early-morning radio — the 8 o'clock news on Sabbath morning. Reminds me of the little battered radio in Pepin's apartment in Madrid. At 7 AM Emilio turns it on to hear the news. In Spanish I understand something of the news. Now, here, it is just tone and rhythm, a spot of music, a morning mishmash, like the sound of the truck going by and the song of the birds.

8:07 AM I have moved to the living room. All is quiet, I am the only one yet awake. So. What have I to tell of the last two weeks? I haven't been very good at writing in this scribble. It has been a quiet, pleasant time. I have stayed about החוף הירק The Green Beach Hotel — why it is called that I don't know. A limited world, a safe world, a structured place. It is a novelistic setting. The 93-year-old ex-general, the Japanese studying Hebrew, the Arab doctor who works in the refugee camps of Gaza, the born-again Christian lady from Florida, the gay tax lawyer from Honolulu, the woman from Bulgaria who has settled into a kibbutz on the Golan Heights — and Humphrey Bogart as the tough, crafty, laconic hotel owner. Yesterday morning as I walked to the beach, two young soldiers in full battle kit came running past me. And then a whole squad along the surf and rifle shots in the sea bluffs to the south.

So — here, in the living room, there is the disorder of life — photo albums, of different shapes, sizes, colors and ages, are piled on the coffee table, along with a plastic bag of crackers, a fork, two knives, a pair of gloves. On a couch a pile of newspapers. I'd like to go out and walk, but I wouldn't be able to get back in, I fear. I have a stoppered feeling. The clouded morning, the silence and disorder. I look at a large electric fan, which sits ten feet from me, in the enclosed balcony. Its head, with the three broad blades behind the wire screen, is bowed and waiting. It stands out in space — alone, surrounded by space. That is the quality — the sensing of that quality can lead to reality, I think.

Rather, I feel. I don't sense it much with human-made objects. I get it most from trees or plants. That stand up into space. This quality of being in space — alone in space — means a lot. I don't often see anything that way. I mostly see things — anything — in relation. To other things. To me. To use or condition. But they all stand alone. They fill space in apparent solidity. No, that's not it. The principal thing is that they are here, at this moment. Standing still. And yet they are in great motion — in time. But when I look at them they are standing still. Everything stands still. Some disagreeably so — like this square dark television set on the platform-shelf in front of me. Why is the TV set disagreeable? The dark color? The dead gray screen? Maybe it is hard to see the TV set as still because it is such a dead solid weight against the dead white wall. The electric fan has the see-through wire screen, the curved and separated blades, the bowed head. I can see it is set to move, is moving, although I see it as standing still. The TV set doesn't move, will never move. Although on top of the TV are two white china swans — their necks curving to form a heart between them. Do they help the TV? No, not much — there is still the dead wall behind them. The fan has the light of day behind it.

I see, out the part-open balcony louvers, the dusty pale red roof and white wall of the house across the street. That is in motion too. It will be out of sight in 30 or 80 years. And the grey white sky? Is it in motion too? Does the sky stand still? The sky changes too often to be in motion, is too universal to stand still. I have very little idea of what I am talking of. And the clock ticks on, and flashes. It is a brass mechanism inside a glass bell. A brass piece revolves and flashes reflected light every second.

Now I am a little hungry. Am I? Or am I just impatient to be doing something that will rattle away the day for me? I am tired of sitting and looking. I want to be occupied. Taken away, made purposeful. The purpose of eating, the purpose of talking, the grand purpose of appearing to be me. Yet it is a great burden — being me. What would it be like to not be me? I am a camera — that phrase comes to me. If I am not me — what do I do? Do I observe, watch, record? Stand here and there? See, eat and piss? How could you be you if I am not me? Is that good — if you are not you? Would the fan be a fan, the TV set a TV set, if I am not me? No, probably not. The TV set would be a ugaboo and the fan a powbam. Ugaboo and powbam and no me. Is that a world? And God. Is a ugaboo in his image? His image. Its image? Maybe God is a ugaboo too. Sacrilege. Who says? I don't know. But I think God will get you for this. But — if there is no me, how can he get me? I will have no address. No place to which to address lightning bolts. But he will get your fan and TV set. Don't care. Not at all. No me, no TV, no fan.

A noise, a door opens. The day is soon to begin. Me comes forth, settles into the folds of my shirt, the wrinkles in my pants. Yes? No? An auto goes by in the street below. A toilet flushes. So. Another door opens. Another auto goes by. And another. Another door opens. The brass clock goes round and round. The sound of the water tap. And the water going down the drain. Tap of a toothbrush, smell of soap. The sky is brighter.

50

～ *9* ～

Train to Jerusalem

Clouds are more portentous here

Netanya   Sunday, October 29, 7:55 AM
Just a line to start the day. A bright day by the sea.
Light, sea, birdsong. And starting another week at school
— I love going to school. Life is a school. Theme of the
day.

10:59 AM   The bell rings but I am the only one yet in
the classroom. Flies flit and sunlight yipeedays in bright
spots on the orange and yellow chairs.

Netanya   Tuesday, October 31, 3:31 PM
Okay — so here we are. Dr. Sadowitz, dentist, 39
Disengoff St. — go to the back entrance. I did. Door
locked. So now I sit outside the building, by the narrow
flagstone walkway to the back entrance. I sit on a low
stone wall. Wearing a hat — Me, dental patient — a half
hour early. Why? Because my gums started bleeding a
few days before I left Santa Cruz. This I do not ignore —
since teeth pulled, gums cut away, last April. So I made
an appointment and I shall see Dr. Sadowitz, God
willing. I have traveled נוסע to downtown Netanya נתני

by bus ‏באוטובוס‎. And I write. ‏ואני כותב.‎

5:48 PM   On the bench at the Central Bus Station. Almost an hour ago I ran up to a bus, looked around the front to see the lighted #7 sign and got on. The bus went on, people on and off, and — it came back to the Central Bus Station, never coming close to the Green Beach Hotel. So now I wait for what I hope is the real #7.

5:54 PM   On the bus again. As I handed the driver the fare, I said Ze sheva, lo? (This is Seven, no?) He may have moved his head, he may not have. It doesn't look like the previous bus #7s I've been on, but the fare, 2.80 shekels, is the same. So. I shall see.

Netanya   Thursday, November 2, 8:09 AM
Away — on the magic taxicab carpet. Away from the sea, away from Ulpan Akiva. Into the dark clouds shielding the morning sun. White tall buildings, highway, morning news on the radio. I chew an orange toothpick. Factory buildings, grey metal on the tan soil. Electric substation being built, a boy — white T-shirt, white kippa (skullcap) walking at the side of the highway. An orange grove — my goodness — where is the rail station? We have left the city of Netanya. Perhaps the railroad existed before Netanya. That seems likely — I think the rail line was built by the Germans for the Ottomans. Now we turn off the highway.

8:28 AM   On the train. Southward, ho. To Tel Aviv — 20 minutes. Then we take another train to Jerusalem. I love trains. This is travel. Across the green and living land, past an orange grove. It is true, you know, that automobiles cannot travel across living land. First the land must be killed, then the auto can cross it. For autos are embodied ego (speaking a bit hyperbolically).

The land here lies pleasant under mild morning. This is not the wasteland of the Judean hills or the bustle bam bam of buildings along the highways. Here, Lawrence of Arabia will come galloping from out a lane bordering an orange grove. Yelling Yip ee ii ow ii ay. Or is that John Wayne and the stagecoach? Nelson Eddy? One doesn't know, the pictures of the mind don't match.

There are many soldiers in this train. The army is the nation. Lawrence of Arabia won't capture this train. Ah, white homes, red tile roofs. We may be coming to Aix-en-Provence. No dusty oasis, this. Now the banks of apartments pyramiding back to catch the sun.   The cars are full. This is a commuter train. Carrying a commuter army. A young fellow walks by, his submachine gun clicking against his belt. We pass a gravel loading area. A wall of rose oleanders. A screen of eucalyptus, a bright green field. A highway is now alongside. Oil storage tanks. The fellow across from me wears a knit kippa, reads a paperback book. Is it in English? I can't quite make out the cover words.

9:18 AM   Tel Aviv station. On the train to Jerusalem. Very few passengers on this one. I am traveling today with two other people from the Ulpan: Mary, who was in my class, and Fong, who is in a more advanced class. Mary from Florida, Fong from Singapore. As I sit in the coach, the cars wizz by on the expressway alongside the station.

9:36 AM   Off we go — six minutes late. Past the chunky white buildings of Tel Aviv. Coca-Cola — red — on top of a building. Under a fresh-built expressway.

Dusty green trees — a touch of desert color. What we used to call castor oil plants, big many-pointed leaves, growing on the roadbed cut. Now, open fields, houses in the middle distance, far off now, the towers of Tel Aviv. New houses, in all stages of construction, marching across the land. The train now going lickety split. Smooth roadbed. Off on the right (I'm sitting backwards) the huge flat-topped mound that is the Tel Aviv refuse dump. Orange groves. White and red houses. Above them, towering grey and white clouds. Clouds are more portentous here. This morning I walked out the gate of the hotel and looked up to see broad beams of white light issuing from behind a band of black cloud on the eastern horizon. Is this It? Someone talking to me? A romantic thought? Nineteenth century? CE or BCE?

9:55 AM   I just peed. I could see the rail ties whizzing by through the bottom of the toilet. Olive grove. And beyond, like a mirage, brand-new, stark white high-rise apartment buildings. Lod station. Peace reigns on the rail line. "Ramale is the next stop" says a voice.

10:03 AM   This must be Ramale.

10:08 AM   Out the right side, dark flat fields, and in the distance black hills against billowing grey clouds.   We are going up to the holy city. The land has opened up and begins to swell. Green orchards over the bosom, high dry grass along the roadbed, a eucalyptus forest.

10:18 AM   Now the train began to swing around a curve. We are moving into the swells. Rich brown soil, plowed and bare. A pecan? orchard. Higher and higher the pregnant swells. The train lurches, sways. It is harder to write. A small hill thickly planted with trees, stately, reaching to the sky. The train slows, labors. Higher the swells. A thick orchard — oranges? No. Shadow and sunlight. The steady complex click of the wheels on the rails, the stretch and rumble of the cars. The sky suddenly opens and I sit in full bright sunlight. Smell of diesel smoke. To the right, a quarter-mile, a steep hill, almost an escarpment, a group of white houses strung out along its base. Long sheds near the track. Through an opening, I see a great flock of white birds. The voice announces a station. I don't catch the name. I ask Fong. Shemesh, he says.

It is 10:32. A small concrete building alongside the track, the shutters painted bright violet. An industrial building. Looks like the cement factory at Davenport, north of Santa Cruz. The train squeaks and shrieks around a curve. High rock hills directly ahead. The hillside by the track strewn with large white rocks. Here is a great cut in the hill — limestone for the cement plant? The track now follows the way of a narrow gorge in the hills, an ascending arroyo or wadi. We are close confined — this is the steep and narrow path. To the holy city. A baby makes sounds: Ala ala ala ala. The gorge opens. A round watchtower. Looks like a fortification — gun ports. The steep and rocky hillsides are spotted with small green bushes. They look planted. I think I hear a silent Hallelujah beyond the rickety click of the train. Why is that?

The hills may be mountains. A cut rock wall along the uphill side of the track. I switch seats, to the downhill side. Yes, this narrow track, this working train. I look down to the bottom of the gorge. Do I see water? Yes, yes. A small mountain stream. How delightful — to see water in this high dry land. The stream is not much more than a yard across, but there is a swift and curling current. A dirt road crosses the little stream, on an arched stone bridge. Here is a high hill planted to evergreens. The green and the water lift my spirit. Water and life. I wonder if the stream is constant or if the water now is from the rains of last night? Maybe it is raining even now up ahead.

Now it is 10:54 AM — only 20 minutes from Jerusalem station if we are on time. No sign of habitation in this steep and narrow path. Only the rail line — a single track — and the little stream. Another hillside forest. The valley opens out. There is an olive grove on the flat bottom land. Several miles of olive orchard alongside the track — some of it on carefully made stone-walled terraces. Ah — a stone village up above the tracks. A kitchen garden. Now, a few miles past the village, I see many stone terraces, in disrepair, with no trees or only dead trees. Time gone, trees gone. A stony land, it needs attention. Oh my — a hill full of modern cliffside apartments. Are we approaching the city? The voice makes an announcement. Ah — on a far hill, a great spreading white wall of cliffside apartments. The train stops. Two men stand outside — one talks into a cellular phone. Another young man, wearing civilian clothes and one earring, stands near them with a submachine gun. Submachine guns seem as common as cigarette lighters here. Almost.

It is 11:11 AM — four minutes before our scheduled arrival. Why have we stopped here? Maybe one can't simply roll into Jerusalem. Maybe it is a time for prayer. Ah — we start again. Very slowly. We cross a conduit — a water course? Past the bare rock ground. Ah, a large white building. Is that the Knesset building? Don't know.

We are suddenly in the city. A sports stadium? Power
lines.   Now a city panorama ahead — white houses
across a broad hillside. We cross under a highway. A
grove of dead olive trees. Another underpass.   Old stone
building. New stone building. A mosque tower. Is this
an Arab village on the outskirts? Looks like a school,
next to the mosque. Now we pass the backsides of big
city buildings — warehouses?   We pass apartments,
buildings, streets — we are in mid-city. The train horn
sounds every few seconds. We slow. I think we have
arrived — at 11:21 AM.

∽ *10* ∾

Jerusalem

Have I enough hair to fashion myself religious?

Jerusalem   Still Thursday, 5:47 PM
Standing against a low stone wall on Bar Kochba
Street. Why? I am early. It is a wonder I arrived. It
was 20 questions. Where can I catch the #4 bus? Where
is Bar Kochba Street? The driver said Ani lo yodea — I
don't know. I asked an old fellow across the aisle: First,
Do you speak English? A little, he said. Bar Kochba
street? I said. What number? he said. Nine. Ah, he said
and put up his index finger — meaning no problem.
Several blocks later he motioned. Here, he said — across
the street, go up the stairs. I did, looked at the first
apartment building. Yes — a lighted Number Nine.
But no apartment 18 — from the mailboxes there were
only 12 apartments. I stopped a fellow on the street.
Fluently, he said to my first question. Yes, he said, this is
Bar Kochba, but number nine is on the other side of the
street. It was a project to cross the street because the two
sides of the street are at different levels. I got across —
number 11 — walked a bit further — number 13. Turned
around — the next entrance had no number, I continued
on. A man came out of the next building. No, he said, this

is number five — so I went back to the dark entrance — all the names on the register are in Hebrew. I puzzled the last one out to be almost Hertzberg — it ends with a qof instead of a gimmel. But I'll go back now and push that button.

Jerusalem   Friday, November 3, 7:21 AM

Breakfast. A click of plates, gurgle of a refrigerator. Sweet rice puffs and cream. Not what the doctor ordered, but the doctor is not in my tent, for I dwell among the puff-rice-ites. Verily. I look for tea. Verily. And there is but coffee. I drink sweet orange water by the hotel called Menorah.   I have been reading the Bible before breakfast. Abram, who became Abraham, and Sarai to Sarah. And the Pharaoh. Cast of thousands. Fire and brimstone.

The sun sits on the back of my neck. Not a trifle — the Jerusalem sun. God's own sun. I am soon off again to talk with David. We have set a schedule for the next two weeks.   The older couple a few tables away are pointing, speaking English. Everyone speaks English. The populace of Jerusalem is American. Little known fact. More Americans than Edomites, Jebuzites, Canaanites, or Philistines. Teenagers, mothers and babies, tottering elders, the man in the street: when they open their mouths they say American. Oh, there are Israelites, Arabs, Armenians — of course. But they are in rock caves, stone buildings — the streets are American.

8:31 AM   Autobus Arbah (4) — that's what I was going to ask for. But I saw the sign with the 4 upon it.

8:34 AM   On the bus. Got the last seat. A covey of nice teenage girls in front of me. Going to high school. Me too.

Going to school. Past the stone buildings, a green park. The city relaxes in the sun, cars move at a stately pace, the trees reach up to heaven. Even the music is dreamy instead of rack-a-rock-a-boom. Morning in Jerusalem, the city of the hills. Gone are the cities of the plain, the city on the hills abideth. Liveth, bideth, sitteth in the bus-eth and goeth forth to worketh, etcetereth, etcetereth. Autos are parked on the sidewalk — something they must have learned from the French. Here we are going through Mea Sharim — a neighborhood of religious done in collaboration between God and the Ministry of Tourism. I wonder if I still have enough hair to fashion myself religious? Religion takes lots of hair. Unless your hair runs wild, your soul is not free. It is the medium — hair — that gives the message. Long hair, long coat. I could get a wig — long curly black hair with dripping black side curls. Achad Ha Pious, I would call myself. Well — I must begin looking for Bar Kochba — the street.

12:40 PM I think it's called the Village Green. The restaurant. I am up on the balcony. Overlooking. And eating lentil soup. A mess of potage. Or is it a pot of message? I have done a semi-nutty morning. With my teacher, the hippie Talmudic sage, out of 1970s San Francisco. First we talked on the roof as he hung his laundry. From the roof I saw — ha harim shel Yarushelaim — ההרים של ירושלים — the mountains of Jerusalem. King David said in every direction he saw them. And on the horizon, the tower on top of the hill is the tomb of Samuel. Then we sat down and talked of this week's portion of the Torah: the Lord said to Abram Go yourself from your land, from your birthplace, from the house of your father, to a land I shall show you. The first word ויאמר as I remember it. David — my teacher David — asked What does it mean? What do the three letters אמר mean? Well, I said, that looks like omer, which means "to say". Yes, he said, but the yod (י) at the beginning makes it the future tense — "he will say". And there is something else you will find only in the Torah. A special way of communicating — as lovers communicate with special ways of saying things. Only in the Torah, when there is a vav (ו) in front of the verb it reverses the time. If the verb is in the future time, as here, it becomes the past. When in the past, it becomes the future. So this word, "he will say", becomes "he said". Why is this done? Well, I said, to merge past and future. Yes, he said, God does not do in time. It says: In the beginning he created, but he is still creating today. We do not read the Torah for history, we read to find what we should do today. Later, he said: God, the Torah, the land, and the Jew are one. (Did he include God in the quartet?) We, you and I, are sitting here discussing the Torah — as Jews have done for 3000 years. (Did he say 2000?) We are communicating, discussing the oral tradition. The Torah is entering us, we are becoming one with it.

I stop writing, look down at the floor below this balcony, the door leading to Ben Yehuda Street (a pedestrian street), the tables set out in front of the restaurant. If a bomb is thrown in? I look at the back of the balcony. There, and I shall throw myself on my face under a table. But the smoke? No air to breathe.

Let's look at this one sentence, he said. Look at this one word לך-לך lech-lcha. Lech is a form of the verb to walk or to go — the command form. Lcha means "to you". Why say "to you"? — it is already in the verb. Well, I said, it is emphasis — as in English you can say Go, but you can also say You go, for more emphasis. In the Torah, he said, there are at least four levels, summed up in the word פרדס pardes (or paradise), which means orchard. And he told me the words each of the four letters of פרדס (pardes) is the initial letter of, but I cannot remember them. Peh (פ) is the simple level. Here, the simple meaning of the word is You go. Rosh (ר) is the level of hint or intuition — one word to a wise man. Here, lech-lcha is Go to you. Go to yourself. Go out from what you know — your land, your birthplace, your father's house — and find yourself.

On the third level, the dalet (ד), the sages often explain with a parable or a story. Rabbi _____ of Chernobyl (Chernobyl? I said in my head) told this story: There was a learned and pious rabbi, who through an error, a misjudgment, was put in prison. He was put in a cell with an old man. Why has this happened to me? he asked. Do you really want to know? asked the old man — then think — what has been your work that you most delight in? Yes, said the rabbi, collecting money to help those in prison. God is helping you, said the old man, to do this better. Before you did it very well, but now you will know yourself what it is like to be in prison, and you will do your work better. So, David asked, do you see how this explains what God said to Abraham? No, I said. What was Abraham known for, what was his delight? I looked blank. It does not come out until a later chapter, he said. Oh yes, I said — hospitality — as when he invited the angels into his tent, slaughtered an ox, so on. And I got it. Abraham was to be a stranger, a wanderer in a far land. It is only when you have been homeless yourself, said David — that you know what it is. And he talked of hitchhiking across the US with only $11 in his pocket. I found myself then moved almost to tears by the story of the Rabbi of Chernobyl.

You know what we can do today? said David. We can spend ten minutes more on this sentence and then we can go to visit the tomb of Rachel in Bethlehem. Have you been to Bethlehem?   No, I said, I'd like to do that. Tomorrow, he said, is the day on which Rachel died and there will be thousands going to her tomb.   Rachel's tomb is in the middle of the road. When the Jews were sent to exile in Babylonia, they passed the tomb and heard Rachel crying. But the Torah says — and he quoted the Hebrew — something about there is always hope.

Well, the fourth level, the samech (ס), is the secret level. You know that each Hebrew letter is also a number. Lamed (ל) is 30 and kaf (ך) is 20 — so (לך-לך) lech-lcha is 50 and 50. When did Abraham die?   I don't remember, I said.   175, he said, and how old was he when he left Ur of the Chaldees?   75, I said.   So he had 100 years of life left and that is contained in lech-lcha. And how old was Abraham when Isaac was born?   100, I said. And then he talked of the intricate correspondence between letters and words in the Torah that is being discovered by computer analysis now.

Wow, I am tired — it is 2:10 PM now. I shall tell of the trip to Bethlehem later.

[A 2017 memory: I never wrote in this long letter of the trip to Bethlehem. Bethlehem is Arab, across the line between Israel and the Palestinian territory, and, yet, it is in the same city as Jewish Jerusalem. We got there with a taxi ride through city streets; it was like going from downtown Santa Cruz to Capitola. We drove through an Arab neighborhood and arrived at Rachel's tomb, an ancient stone structure set in the street, armed Israeli soldiers and military vehicles about it. David led me inside. It was dark, cave-like and unbreathably packed with men — mostly young — wearing dark suits, black fedoras or skullcaps and long sidecurls. David pushed his way through the crowd into an inner room and towed me along. I felt quite uncomfortable, physically and emotionally — I had no idea about what the be-suited men were doing, or what I was to do, there. What hit me most about the whole thing was the bizarre confluence of the armed soldiers and the another-time, another-country haredim (ultra-orthodox).]

Historical photo of Rachel's Tomb

64

∿ *11* ∿

The Western Wall

Bar Mitzvah at 65

Still Friday, 2:44 PM   Waiting. One of my lessons in
the Ulpan was about waiting in Israel. Here one waits,
was the theme. I forget the verb. But "line" (as in wait-in-
line) in Hebrew is "tor" תור. I actually know a lot of verbs.
The infinitives begin with ל — the lamed, which means
"to". Example: "to do" — לעסות.

3:21 PM   Oh my. I have died and gone to hotel heaven
— here at the hostel/hotel Beit Shmuel. It is a long story.
But now — and perhaps for the whole two weeks I am
in Jerusalem, I have a gem of a room. I see that it has
fold-down beds so it can sleep six — but now it is set up
with just one queen-size bed — all modern Danish, ship-
shape decor. And beyond the window is a wide step-out-
on balcony with a view of the walls of the Old City. Throw
in a 15 cent sample size shampoo and it would be $200 at
the King David Hotel, up the street a bit. I pay but $45
for this. The story is that I booked a room two weeks ago.
When I arrived yesterday, they had screwed up, canceled
my reservation and given my room to another. I agreed
to go to another place last night — Hotel Menorah, two

blocks away. I guess this room is a recompense.

10:03 PM   Tomorrow — tomorrow I am going to be Bar
Mitzvah-ed by the holy rollers. Have I mentioned that?
My hippie Talmud sage decided this.

I went tonight to the Western Wall to pray with the
Shlomo Carlebach contingent of Jerusalem — praying
with a yippy-ai-oh. Clapping, dancing in circles and lines,
singing, voices bouncing off the rock wall. I wasn't with
it. I couldn't understand it.

After praying at the Western Wall, the group went to
the Shlomo Carlebach Center and I stayed for supper. It
wasn't horrible but I would have preferred to be walking
or scribbling or reading. I sat across from Meyer, a nice
middle-aged man from England, And on one side of me
was a fellow about 25 with a reddish-brown beard who
last Wednesday did Aliyah (became an official immigrant
to Israel). He is from Los Angeles and is an instructor in
Jewish karate, which he says has a number of centers
in Southern California. Last year he went to Alaska for
three months to work on a fishing boat. Cold, hard work,
little sleep, fights, injuries — the only thing that saved
him, he said, was the peace he had on reciting some
prayers to himself on Sabbath. That's when he decided to
come to Israel.

On the other side of me was a thin young man with
curly black hair named Moshe. How many languages
do you speak? he asked me in heavily accented English.
English, Spanish and French, I said — and you? English,
he said, and Russian. When we sat down at the table
there were little serving bowls of hummus, carrot salad,
tahini and that eggplant dish which is eaten here. Moshe

reached for every bowl after it had been passed about and spooned out all the remainder on his plate. Then he reached over to the other tables and got their serving bowls and did the same. When the big plate of garlic-roasted potatoes came around, Meyer, the fellow on the other side, said "not too much, Moshe, not too much" as Moshe pushed potatoes onto his plate. But when the main dish of boiled fish came around, Moshe didn't take any of it.

After the meal, David, my teacher, said: This week's portion is lech-lcha — about Abraham being told by God to leave Ur of the Chaldees. So, he said, let us go around and each person tell in a few words how they came to Israel. I'll begin, he said. And then he talked for 15 minutes, rambling on about San Francisco, his wife who didn't want to come to Israel, his daughter, so on and so on. Then a young woman spoke briefly.

Then a fellow sitting at a table in the women's section said, I want to speak. (Yes, there is a room partitioned off by lace curtains where the women sit during the services — a very disagreeable feature). So this fellow said, I don't know why I can't leave Israel. I left Chicago, he said, because I killed my stepfather and stepmother and they wanted to put me in prison. And he talked in that off-the-moon-and-flying manner for another five minutes. David tried to lighten the mood by wisecracking. This ordinary-looking fellow with off-the-ceiling stories is apparently not new at the Center.

Jerusalem   Saturday, November 4, 7:25 AM

Bright morning, quiet morning. I am going down to breakfast — where I am to meet Regan, a Norwegian woman who was in my class at Ulpan Akiva in Netanya.

Then to the Bar Mitzvah — which I am of a mind to cancel. I don't feel it appropriate for me now. I do not know enough yet.

1:10 PM   Not changed by Bar Mitzvah, I am at lunch. The restaurant Select in the Armenian quarter. Happy. To be away, to be alone. At the next table I hear French — that is a good omen. To be away? From my new congregation.

Street view of Select Restaurant in the Armenian quarter

I came to the Western Wall at 9:15 this morning. Saw no one I knew from last night. Then came the tall stout fellow in the long black satin coat and the brown fur hat. An exotic figure — but from America, and a doctor. He is also the head of the Shlomo Carlebach Center. He greeted me and I said, I do not want to do the Bar Mitzvah this morning.   Do you know what a Bar Mitzvah is? he asked.   No, I said, that is the problem.

My salad arrives, with a round of pita bread.

Mitzvah, he said, you know what that means? Yes, I said, a good deed. Bar, he said, means something like

accepting responsibility for doing mitzvah. You don't
have to know anything to do Bar Mitzvah — only be
willing to accept that responsibility. At 13, a boy, at 12,
a girl, takes on that responsibility. A boy at 13 can come
up to read the Torah.   I can't read Hebrew, I said.   My
father, he said, did not become observant until he was
60. At 80 he was ordained a rabbi by Shlomo Carlebach.
My grandfather, he said, was a Bundist from Odessa, so
my father received no religious education as a boy. My
father lived in Arizona and he saw there was no Jewish
chaplain at the prison. So he began going there, and they
questioned his status, so Shlomo ordained him a rabbi. It
was one of the happiest days of his life — he died a year
later. Bar Mitzvah is just you saying you are an adult
Jew and the community marking its acceptance of you as
part of it.

Later, David, my hyperactive Talmud sage, brought me a
book with the brief blessings I would say at the Bar
Mitzvah. As the service went on I read them and
matched the Hebrew to the English translation. I saw
verbs I already knew like נתר — "he gave".   Then — for
the Torah reading — we left the Western Wall, and went
up to the two small white rooms they have rented as the
Center.

Four Americans come in the front door of the restaurant.
Welcome, says the manager, who holds the door open.
No smoking, one man says. Far away as possible, says a
woman. I look at the French at the next table. Yes, two of
them are smoking. I hadn't noticed.   Oh my, outside is
a procession of men in long black robes with black cowls
— sort of a Ku Klux Klan-looking group. There go the
Armenians, says one of the Americans behind me.

The Western Wall

This morning, the service at the wall was quieter than last night. And, at the Center, I did the Bar Mitzvah, which consisted only of reciting the blessings for the reading of the Torah. The week's Torah portion is divided into seven parts, and there is a blessing before and after each part. The reading was done by a gnarled old guy who looked as if he hadn't shaved for a few days. I held his hand as we danced in a circle later and his was the tough hand of someone who does hard labor. The dancing was after I said the blessings. Things rained upon my shoulders and head. Hard candies. Then David began singing and clapping and we joined hands, singing: simcha ve mazel tov — happiness and congratulations (or good luck).

As I said the blessings, David coached me in an

undertone, and asked me if I would sponsor the kiddush.
Pay? I said, yes. I grasp meanings in a sketchy way.
Kiddush, I thought, was the snacks after the service. And
it was. Grape juice, some sort of baklava, pickled herring
and black olives.   Then they set the food table to one side
and started praying again. It was about 12:30.   I sidled
toward the door. The doctor in the black satin and the
fur hat came up. You are staying for lunch? he asked, it
will be only ten minutes. So I remained. And the praying
went on. I wished fervently I had said I had to return to
my hotel for some previously arranged meeting. But I
had not wit or insincerity enough.

Yes — now a camel passes outside this restaurant.

6:27 PM   At a table outside a dairy restaurant on a
walking street.

7:56 PM   Same table. I came, I ate, I wrote a letter. I
also read several pages of Hebrew in a textbook I bought
at the Ulpan in Netanya.

Jerusalem   Sunday, November 5, 7:47 AM
Breakfast at Beit Shmuel. I first took from the buffet
table some small pancakes and a fried egg. Aarg —
greasy kid stuff.   Now I have fetched myself a plate of
tomato, cucumber, green pepper and cottage cheese and
a couple slices of rye bread. A better way to breakfast.
This morning, in this dining room, there are but a third
as many people as there were at this time yesterday.
People at breakfast in hotel dining rooms almost always
are silent, subdued, timid. Something about being
untimely thrust before the world?

Or is that just me? Actually, I feel a bit of nervous

bravado. But physically I feel not yet fully formed for the day. There are still nerves ringing and unrested, saying daylight, shmaylight, we are still not ready. Why? I have taken to drinking tea since I've been in Israel — I am now having my second breakfast cup. Could I be caffeinated? Needing a little jolt of caffeine to calm the nerves? But, caffeine is not a calmer, it is a zig-a-zag a-boom-a-rater.

My mind wanders. I am content to be a schlump in Jerusalem. I don't want to take a cab to see the Golan Heights, I don't want to go scuba diving at Eilat, I don't want to walk in ancient water tunnels under old Jerusalem. I like to float, not drill, into a place, a city.

11:38 AM Lost. And found. Panoramic view. Swedish (or Dutch?) tourists at the table behind me, all wearing identical white kibbutz caps. I was looking for two places Menny (the professor who guided the Ulpan Akiva group through the Old City ten days ago) said not to miss. I can't remember what they were — maybe one a synagogue, the other a museum. I picture perfectly how they were —one inside an arched entry, the other, opposite, down a stone lane. But I haven't found the place in 40 minutes of wandering in the Old City — up stone, down stone, around stone — and I don't know what to ask for. So I settled for a glass of orange pop and a seat in the shade. And the panoramic view. If the ruined walls just down-stone from me were cleared off, I think I would see the Western Wall.

What would I call myself? The accidental tourist? Accidental, incidental, immaterial, evanescent and gone? Could be. This morning, I set out with my shoulder bag, heavily freighted by my — what? four pound? — Torah in

Hebrew, English and with commentary. I wanted a sane and quiet place to read. I reached the sidewalk in front of Beit Shmuel, my hospice/hotel. Crazy, I said, to walk a mile with this — there is the lovely courtyard of Beit Shmuel. So I went back and read the Torah portion I am to discuss with my hyperactive Talmud sage this evening — starting at Abraham greeting the angels of the Lord as they go to Sodom, and reading on to Abraham ready to kill Isaac. It is a worked-over story, snippets and bits told and retold again. So what do centuries of rabbis — the million books of commentary — make of it?

12:55 PM   Eating lunch — at the same Panorama Café. Somewhere in the distance the sound of a jackhammer — the nervous stutter of progress. I have sat here, at Panorama Café, reading the early pages of this screed. I feel heartened — it's not totally stupid — I find it interesting. No — I see from the napkin this is not the Panorama Café. It is the Quarter Café — panoramic view, self-service etc. So — when it comes right down to it — I don't give a damn about being a tourist.

But, I say: Do I not eat my coleslaw as you eat coleslaw? The rice, the pita bread, the chicken soup? If I walk your stone steps, do I not tire? If lost, am I not anxious?   So what? says another voice within.   I am a human being, I say, not a tourist.   That's what they all say, he says — the stout lady in the blue T-shirt, the Swedish girl who told you This is the women's room, when you came out of the toilet stall.   She was wrong, I say — there is only one bathroom here.   That's not the point, he says, she also says she is human.   So she is, I say.   You see, he says, all tourists are also human beings.   Oh my, I say, I didn't realize that. And soldiers, he says, nursemaids, miners, scuba divers.

I look up — I raise my eyes — to the panorama. That is East Jerusalem, the hill, the valley beyond the Temple Mount. It is all one city. Friday, when we went to Bethlehem, the driver said it was three miles from Jerusalem. Closer than Capitola to Santa Cruz. How can it be divided? How can the people live in peace? I am afraid my hippie sage is waiting for the Third Temple to rise on the Temple Mount. There is a line between religious ecstasy and lunacy like the line between Jerusalem and Bethlehem.

A Jerusalem panorama

A flock of people pass, speaking Russian. They don't look like Jews. Russians have been released from their vast prison.

4:33 PM Sitting in the courtyard of Beit Shmuel. I have washing going in the machine downstairs. Now I want to go over the Abraham story again — at six I am meeting with David again.

5:25 PM Waiting for the #4. In front of a ziggurat. It might be a hotel also. It is black night. The air is oxygen, nitrogen and auto-gen. A bus labeled 4H pulls up. Shall I take it or hold out for the pure 4? I decide on purity, since I am a stranger in the land. All sorts of buses come by this stop — 9, 48, 14 — pick a number. But no 4, as yet. I think — what questions do I have about those Torah passages? I feel as if I have not completed my homework. I was to write down questions. A man wearing a dark suit and open-necked white shirt leans over me (I am sitting on a bench), says something I don't understand, puts two fingers to his mouth as if smoking. I shake my head. He does the same thing to the young woman sitting at the other end of the bench, a baby on her lap. What he spoke sounded more like Russian than Hebrew.

❧ *12* ❧

A Terrible Day

As the sirens begin, I find I am crying

Still Sunday, 5:36 PM On the bus. The driver has a talk program on the radio, tuned up loud. Hey, that's my kind of radio — if it is an intelligent program. I hear Rabin's name mentioned. Rega, says a man. I understand that — it means "wait".

8:45 PM Well, I have been on planet X, not earth, today. When I came up the stairs, David was outside his door. This is a terrible day, he said — one of the worst in the history of this country. Why? I said. You haven't heard? he said. No, I said. Rabin, the prime minister, has been assassinated. I have had no hint, all day. No one appeared to me to be agitated today.

8:49 PM Now on the bus. Two young men in full battle kit, carrying the ever-present submachine guns, get on. This driver also has the radio on — to talk. Now I understand why — there is probably no music on Israeli radio today. Still — no one seems in a state of shock — as I remember the US when Kennedy was killed. David said: It is because people here go on, have learned to go on, no matter what.

Jerusalem   Monday, November 6, 7:14 AM
Breakfast, in the dining room of Beit Shmuel. There is no somber-ness at all here this morning so far as I can tell; no one is talking of the assassination. I walked up to the King David Hotel 20 minutes ago to buy a newspaper. There were police and barricades and a big army van outside and troupes of dark suits and briefcases inside.

9:03 AM   After reading in the paper that the funeral is at 2 PM and respects are being paid in the courtyard of the Knesset, I called David and canceled our meeting at 1 PM today. I decided to walk to the Knesset, got a bit lost, came upon a corner where hundreds of candles were placed in little cans on the sidewalk and on walls, many with notes stuck under the cans.   I asked a boy, Does this have to do with Rabin?   Yes, he said, this is the house where he lives.

9:36 AM   I am on the street that leads to the Knesset. Crowds of people walk up and look, mostly school kids. I don't see on their faces shock or sorrow. But yes, a woman now goes by — she has been crying.

9:53 AM   I sit on a bench in a park adjacent to the Knesset. There seems no organized way of going by the casket in respect. People have come up into the park, looking through the iron palisade fence to the Knesset forecourt below — it is a puzzled, quiet crowd. On the next bench over sit four young soldiers — high school kids, each with his own submachine gun.

10:05 AM   I have been walking away from the Knesset on a path in this lovely rose garden. And now I sit on a bench in the shade alongside the path. The path is bordered by large spice plants. I crush a sprig and smell. Rosemary. Or thyme? This is a nice place to come on a better day. I tire of Torah study. Not that I have done any. The fellow who killed Rabin is a law student at Bar Ilan University in Tel Aviv, described in the paper as very intelligent, gentle and an intense Torah student. Here comes a helicopter low-in, directly toward me — now it veers off to the Knesset building, now circles back and comes in even lower. It is landing. So — there is this impulse, this attitude, of some people who call themselves religious, which is so horribly arrogant.

The Knesset Menorah in Wohl Rose Park in front of the Knesset building

10:45 AM   I have given up all hope. Therefore, I begin to enjoy. I have no idea where I am or how to arrive at a familiar place. So I sit in the stone lobby of a stone building and drink cold grapefruit juice. My life is sitting and drinking cold grapefruit juice. And my life is good. A

tall man wearing a fluorescent orange cap runs by. Now
he runs back. There goes another kid with a submachine
gun. Maybe this one is only an automatic rifle.   The
woman at the next table leans toward me. Spakisih
Ruski? she says.   Ruski? I say, — ingles — she looks at
me.   Française? I say, espanol?   Oh, frances, she says.
I begin writing again. At the table at my other side there
is a shrill ringing. The young man picks up a cellular
phone and talks. You are nobody in Jerusalem without a
cellular telephone.   The woman at the table on the other
side leaves, then comes back with a bag of potato chips
and — snap crackle crunch — munches.   So. I shall walk
on. The potato chip woman talks to the telephone man.
In Hebrew, I think. I guess she saw me writing in this
peculiar flowing script and she thought it was Russian.
Most non-Hebrew speakers in Israel today are Russians.
So — onward to the warm sun street.

12:03 PM   I eat Italian. She first handed me the Hebrew
menu. I sit outside — this is old modern Jerusalem
— give it 150 years. I went first to the vegetarian
restaurant I was at on Friday. Closed for national
mourning, said the sign posted to the door. So I walked
down this narrow pedestrian street to the Kurdish
restaurant I passed the other evening; it too was closed,
a sign in Hebrew on the door. Then I came around the
corner to this place, which seems mainly pizza. I have
ordered salad and pasta and beer. I shall finish lunch
before the silence at 2 PM. The salad comes, the pasta
comes, a helicopter flies overhead. Another one.

So I eat lunch.   Rabin is dead, the people stroll, buy
books. Whoever built the stone house across this narrow
way is dead too, people ate lunch on the day he or she
died. When I die, you will eat lunch. When you die, I will

eat lunch. I drop some of the salad sauce on my shirt. A woman walks by, her heels clicking on the bricks of the street. Her head, the tilt of her head, hasn't the confidence of the strut of her heels. So all of us: striking a brave note in the world, yet so uncertain inside. A middle-aged American couple sit at the table in front of me. She reads the menu aloud: "pasta, priced by the sauce."

Jaffa Gate and the Tower of David

2:01 PM   I sit on my balcony, looking out at the wall of the Old City and Jaffa gate. At 1:58 the sirens began all over the city. The buses and autos on the road in front of the wall stopped where they were. I find I am crying. It is a sad moment. As the sirens began, a raven flew to the building above me and cawed loudly as long as the sirens wailed. And across the street, from out of the rubble of the construction site, a small cat, spotted white and black, walked to the roadway.

3:02 PM   What's happening? I sit in my room; I feel tired and dispirited. I have lost enthusiasm for studying the Torah — at least with David. I do not look forward to meeting with him tomorrow afternoon. He is not a person I have empathy with. I don't feel like walking about Jerusalem. Of course, I already walked a good five or six miles this morning — out to the Knesset, then to the end of Jaffa Road and back to Ben Yehuda.

I think I shall go the short distance to the Hebrew Union College (of Reform Judaism), which is practically next door.

4:19 PM I sit in a little room downstairs at Beit Shmuel, watching the funeral on TV. The burial ended about a half hour ago. Dignitaries are now filing past the family. Now Clinton is shown entering the Knesset. And I hear helicopters over this place. A cut to Dan Rather being asked by an Israeli newsman — What does this mean to America? Now the screen shows King Hussein arriving at, I think, the King David Hotel, which is only a block from here.

6:22 PM   Eating. At the tiny café in Beit Shmuel. I didn't want to go out in the city. Most restaurants are closed and I feel mostly closed also. The killing of Rabin by a religious nut, the frenzied praying at the Western Wall on Friday night, the touch of weirdness in some of the people at the Shlomo Carlebach Center, the personality of my hippie Talmud sage — all have turned me off to that old time religion. This way of learning, anyway, does not appeal to me.   I think back to the lovely learning of the language at Ulpan Akiva in Netanya. Go back? For eight days of classes? Can it be done? A few hours ago I called a couple ulpans (language schools) in Jerusalem. I talked to someone at the YMCA. ("I learned Hebrew at the YMCA" — an article for National Inquirer?) The woman I talked to didn't think it could be done, but she said to call the teacher, Rachel Cohen רהל כואן tomorrow. The Jerusalem Y is to American YMCAs as the Jerusalem McDonald's is to American Macs. Much more elegant.

There are three young guys chatting in Hebrew at the next table. I pick up words: beseder בסדר, which means "okay" — literally it means "in order" — seder means "order". The Passover Seder is an order of doing things. That is my understanding. These guys are talking of school, I think.

This food I am eating is awful. Three salads on a plate — cabbage and apple, too sweet, olives and pickled vegetables, too hot and salty, eggplant and mayonnaise, too much fat, herb tea, weird taste. But the setting is pleasant. I forgot the three slices of rye bread — just fine. I did walk up a block about 5 PM — to find the World Zionist building, which David told me had a very good restaurant. I asked at the desk and the girl said Walk up to the gas station next to the King David Hotel, go down that street, first you pass the French Consulate, then the Zionist building. I did all that — the gas station, then there was a large stone building behind a high stone wall. The wall sign said Papal Library — something like that. I went on and there was the French Consulate, also behind at a high wall with an iron gate with a sign that says something like Beware, this gate is electrified.

The guy at the next table says shum davar שום דבר which means "nothing". The other guy says rega רגה which means "wait". Yom sheshi יום שישי which means "sixth day" or Friday. Ah, for the good old days when I was a language student.

So — anyway, there was nothing beyond the French Consulate — the road goes round in a half circle, there was some vacant land and then this building, Beit Shmuel. I wonder who Shmuel was?   Beit means "house". It is used in a lot of constructions — like Beit Sefer — "house book", which means school, and Beit Knesset — "house assembly", which means synagogue. Knesset is also the name of the Israeli parliament.   I check the words in the Oxford Hebrew-English dictionary I bought this morning. Shum davar and yom sheshi are okay, but I look up "wait" and don't find rega. So I looked on the Hebrew side. First for the letter Rosh (ר) then the gimmel (ג) and I find it, רגע, but it means "instant, moment", I thought it meant "wait" because our teacher (מורה — mora) always said it when she wanted someone to wait with a question. But she was saying something like "just a moment". And the last letter of rega is an eiyen (ע), not a heh (ה).   There are two silent letters in Hebrew — aleph and eiyen and the heh is almost silent too.   So it's hard to know which one to use.

∾ *13* ∾
Café Tmol Shilshom
I build a life for myself in Jerusalem

Jerusalem   Tuesday, November 7, 10:11 AM
Watching. In a copy shop on Rechov Hillel (rechov means
street). The fellow at the machine in front of me is
copying the first 12 pages of this screed. He doesn't speak
English, so I motion both sides of the paper and five
copies. I know five — חמש — hamesh. But I also put up
five fingers.

This morning I changed course. I called David and told
him I didn't want to continue the lessons with him.
He was very nice. I am absolutely sure I don't want to
continue. I think the major factor is that his personality
does not fit mine.

I look up, on the stairs in front of me the young man has
his hand on the crotch of the young woman. A flashing
second, then they move on. I think they both work here.
I don't think harassment rules have reached Jerusalem.

Anyway, David's very kind attitude during the phone call
increased my trust in him.

A woman talks to me in Hebrew — I look up. Slicha, pardon me, she says, why don't you use a computer? Oh, I say, I write wherever I am. You have a computer? she asks.   Yes, I say, at home — but I would have to carry it with me because I write wherever I am.   She smiles — I wonder, she says, because today people use computers.   So. The fellow is still working on the copies. For some reason the machine didn't do them automatically, so he is laboriously placing each sheet by hand and then turning it over, and laying out each of the five copies. It is taking a long time.

After I called David, I went out — to build a life for myself in Jerusalem. First, I went around the corner — to the Hebrew Union College on David Ha-melech street. The man at the reception desk wore a bright red sweater and spoke British English.   I am here for two weeks and I want to learn about Judaism and Hebrew, I said.   Well, he said, you are starting on two very large projects. The Hebrew courses at the college are six weeks long and already well along — but, he said, the night life of Jerusalem is not as it is elsewhere — here the night life is lectures and talks — get a copy of *This Week in Jerusalem* and *The Jerusalem Post*, they will list what is happening each night.

And, he said, there is a very interesting place, a café. You go down in this direction — and he held out his arm — and there is this old street going up to Jaffa Road with many cafés on it. Yes, I said, I think I know that street. On the right-hand side you will see this sign, and he wrote on a piece of paper CAFÉ TMOL SHILSHOM, there is an arch, you go through the arch and there are several cafés, then you go up a stairway and this

Street view of entrance to Café Tmol Shilshom

café is lined with books, you can read all day there. In the evenings, about seven, there are poetry readings, in Hebrew and other languages.

Also, he said, here in this building we have a museum — it opens at ten — of the artifacts of an excavation at Tel _____, near Dan, you know Israel in ancient times was from Dan to Beersheba. There is a fragment that speaks of King David — it is the first confirmation of David outside the Bible. Also — and this was a Canaanite town — they found a triple arch. You know, it is said the Romans invented the arch, but it is not so — they only popularized it.

After, as I walked down the marble steps of the Hebrew Union College, I pulled from my shoulder bag the frayed sheet of paper on which I had written all the suggestions on Israel I had collected in Santa Cruz. Yes — Café Tmol Shilshom, next to Café Magret — this was a note from who in Santa Cruz?

From Eli, I think, my Hebrew and Judaism teacher. It is a Bohemian place, he said, it is owned by a friend of mine. Later he added, it is something of a gay place too — that was a few weeks later. The Hebrew Union College fellow also said, It is a Bohemian place, like the 1920s, you know.   So — after the bank, and then maybe a haircut.

11 AM   You have to wait, she said. She is counting and recounting a pile of hundred dollar bills. Yes — a bank — the mother's milk of travel. I asked her, can I get shekels here with a Visa card? Yes, she said and waved her index finger at me, but you have to wait.   Naturally — first the money must be counted. Which reminds me of Jesus. The university fellow at the Ulpan said: But of course you had to have moneychangers at the temple. Because an offering had to be made in coins and the foreign coins could not be accepted because they all had graven images on them. So there had to be an exchange to Judean money.

Now, she says, you want?   Five hundred shekels, I say, on my Visa card.   You have your passport? — she speaks English with a French accent. Or, maybe it is a Hebrew accent, they sound similar. This is 175 dollars, she says, the rate is 2.85. You want?   Yes, I say.

11:25 AM   Here we are — zip zut zooie — everything is up to date in Kansas City — you want haircut — here is a salon of hair.

12:29 PM   The Kurdish restaurant — in the dome of the rock — pita bread, eggplant in a sour red sauce, pickled carrots and cucumbers.   I am content.   Since I released myself from my vows of religion, I feel uppity good. I am free to do nothing. Nothing, I am convinced, is the thing to do, the way to go. But what about the 30,000 mitzvahs?

The lentil soup arrives. I like this place very much, my dome of the soul. Only two other customers, two men in pale blue shirts who talk calmly in Hebrew. The soup is very hot, foaming hot in a deep white bowl. The soupspoon is a generous European size so I can zup from the side of it. I am at the nipple, gurgling as I sup my soup and pita bread and golden beer. It is as it is meant to be. Am I thankful?   A Jew is thankful, said David the other night, if he is not thankful he is not a Jew. "Yehuda" means to thank. A Jew thanks God for the food when he eats. When he goes to the bathroom, he thanks God that his organs work so he can do that.   I like that — be thankful. I would like to be thankful. For life, for breath, for awareness, for food, for feet, for eyes and ears, touch and smell, flowers and sky. Do I need for that the rituals and the teaching?

The fish arrives. My oh my — what a picture — a whole trout stretched across the platter, sprinkled over with walnuts and raisins, the platter lined on the top with cucumber slices and on the bottom with tomato and red peppers. The two men have left. A young couple sits at the next table. They speak French. The waitress comes to them.   We are looking at the menu, says the young woman in English. What is a dumpling?   A dumpling? says the waitress, it is bread, uh, I find it hard to explain in English — she turns to me.   Well, I say, it is usually filled with something, like meat and covered with dough.

I eat on — pink trout flesh, eggplant in sour sauce, cucumber and tomato, baked raisins and walnut.   I am becoming too full to be thankful. Food becomes my right, even my burden.   I think of David, my sage. I expected an ethereal type: old man, white beard — somebody from central casting — the Talmudic sage. David is something of a motormouth, streetwise guy, demonstrative. So — call up central casting? Maybe I should have hung on longer? Seen deeper. But he made me nervous, and silent. I was being talked at. During my call this morning, he said, I hope it is nothing I have done?   Oh no, no, I said. I said nothing of personality incompatibility.   I fear I have a tendency to want to blame someone when things don't work out. I didn't do that this morning. But I wasn't frank. The paper said of Yitzhak Rabin yesterday that he always said just where he was and meant what he said. Good quality; I haven't got it. Neither do I deal much with people, especially in difficult situations, where lack of clarity piles up until it breaks something.

I am finishing up my tomato and cucumber salad, and feeling fat and full and unthankful. I think of a nap. I saw the sign for the café — what is its name? Todl Shunshim or something like that. I decided to come here first. Now I think I'll return to Beit Shmuel and come back in late afternoon.   I am staying out of the Old City so far today.   I woke up before six and went out to walk. I turned first to the Old City but after a couple of paces turned back, passed the King David Hotel, went round the corner of the YMCA (called Eemka here) and walked into a quiet, rather elegant neighborhood. Again, and again quite by chance, I walked by the Prime Minister's house. Hundreds of candles were still on the sidewalk, many still burning.

1:38 PM   I asked for the check, now I am waiting,

feeling rather hot and a little impatient. Where is my thankfulness? Comes the check with a little plate with tiny pieces of dried peach. Wow — 70 shekels – the trout is 52 shekels — I thought the menu said 12 shekels. But I guess 52 is right, the meat dishes were 35 or thereabouts. Fortunately, it doesn't mean diddly do.

4:45 PM Here I am. In the promised land. Tmol Shilshom Bookstore Café. Nice place. Would do well in Santa Cruz. In fact, this may be Santa Cruz — somewhere near the university. Everyone is speaking American English. Except the fellow who served my tea — he has a foreign, middle-eastern accent. Nice place — I already said that. It has something of a library look, bookshelves along the walls, good-taste light fixtures. What is that adjective — for good taste? I can't think of it right now. Not cultivated, not discrete, well how about tasteful? That's okay, but there may be another word.

The books in that case behind me are in Hebrew, but near the entrance, they are English. Hey, I twist my neck and look at the books directly at my back. On the shelf is a label in Hebrew: יהדות I spell it out: Ye he dut — could that mean Jewish? I'll thumb through one of the books and see. God — it is hard. It's black on white, patterns of black letters on white paper. I don't get much further than that. The way Hebrew is printed in books, it is hard, almost impossible, to pronounce the words unless you know them personally.

I'll give an example. Here we are on page 212 of the book, second line goes like this:

הסוכות, איש משונה, לבוש, תלבושת מוזרה ותרבוש בראשו.

Now I will transliterate into Roman characters — note that most of the vowels are missing. (And note that I am starting with the first Hebrew word on the right above):

HSOKOT, YSH MSHONA, LBOSH TLBOSHT MOTZRA VTRBOSH BRASHO.

The first H is probably "ha", which means "the". So it is "HA SOKOT" — could that be "The sukkot"? — the holiday or the hut that is built on the holiday? In the second word — the aleph probably is a vowel sound like "ah", so maybe the word is AYESH. "Yesh" means "there is" — but that is spelled without an aleph, like so: יש The ש can either have an S sound or a SH sound. In fully written Hebrew, this is indicated by a dot over the letter — for S it is is written שׂ and for SH is written שׁ — or maybe it is the other way around. And the letter kaf (כ) can have either a K sound or a KH sound (which does not exist in English — it's like this CH in the Scottish "Loch"). In the fully written Hebrew this is indicated by a dot in the middle of the letter (כּ or כ). Same thing with the bet (ב), it can either be B or V, depending on whether there is a dot or not (בּ or ב). Same with the peh (פ) which can be either P or F (פּ or פ).

Then there are all the vowel signs, most of them put under the letters. ֶ and ֵ are pronounced "eh", and ָ and ַ are pronounced "ah", and ִ is "ee". A dot put above and to the left of the letter is "oo", as רֹ would be "roo". But some vowels are represented by letters: the yud (י) often means "ee" and the vav (ו) often means "uh".

Going back to our sentence, I can guess at a couple

words. I think the words לבוש LBOSH and תלבושת TLBOSHT may have something to do with dressing (as in putting on clothes). We learned that verb the last day of class at Ulpan Akiva. Maybe, to tie this together, I can get someone to translate that line. I look at the words again. I will take a further guess. We did not learn the future form of the verbs, but I saw it a few times in my verb book. It may be that the ת (T) in front of TLBOSHT is the future form, and the ת (T) at the end of the word indicates the feminine form. So could it be "she will dress"?

[A 2017 note: Here is how it was translated for me: "The strange Sukkot man wearing a strange outfit and a fez on his head." My analysis was not very good — I should have picked up "ysh" as "man" and seen the letters for "head"(ראש — rosh) in the last word.]

Do I hear thunder outside? Or is it trucks, or handcarts? There are thunderclouds overhead — or were when I walked over here. And it rained while I was napping from about 2:30 to 3:30. So. Maybe. Ooh — I understood a few words from the conversation of two young women a couple tables away. One said "Kitah Aleph" — which means "Class A" — or a beginning class, like the one I was in at Ulpan Akiva. And then she said "bidyuk" — which means "exactly".

5:48 PM   That must have been thunder, because it seems to be pouring rain outside.

6:43 PM   I am supping soup. Very good lentil soup. This is three stars on my personal Jerusalem guide, and in red for pleasant ambience as well. Just before the soup came, I thought of David, I am certainly happier without him. But he was going to introduce me. To God. I must soon leave the party. Of life. And David's friend knows another party. Maybe? Also, being thankful. Maybe he would have shown me how to be thankful. The lentil soup, suddenly, is all gone. The bread too. The music is very pretty here. This is a nice place. I already said that. Twice. I gave the girl who brought my soup, my bookmark from Bookshop Santa Cruz. They have bookmarks from places around the world upon the walls.

Jerusalem   Wednesday, November 8, 6:20 AM
It is a bright clear cold morning outside. I dress quickly. I shall walk before breakfast.

10:58 AM   Tourism. Not all bad. I came here to the Citadel of David at Jaffa Gate and came in because I was waiting for a bus that wasn't leaving until 11. And I find the exhibits quite well done. So I am staying for the guided tour.

1:44 PM   Tired. Very. I just came out of the Tower of David museum. I was there for more than three hours. Rooms, stones, films, maps, pictures, models, holographs: a cracker-jack presentation. Now I am some three centuries down — in the basement, below the street, of the Armenian restaurant I also ate in on Thursday last. Restoring myself with meat soup and Armenian salad and Israeli beer. The only one eating now. My nerve endings are all a-twitch; museums do that to me, they suck the marrow from my bones. Ooh, what an olive — a black olive in my salad, salt of the earth, oil of the earth.

A truck rumble-roars on the street overhead. Not quite overhead. I have a direct sight line to the street. Off the street is an arch. Through the arch is a shop selling jewelry — made, I think by the owner of this restaurant. The shop is on a balcony overlooking the restaurant. So I can look up, see past the shop, out the open door and window, to the street. Fong, my fellow student at Ulpan Akiva, brought me here last Thursday. Fong is a Christian, teaches French and English in Singapore, knows five or six languages, is staying five months at the Ulpan. A captivated Christian. There are many at the Ulpan. Asawa, the Japanese, Mary from Florida. They are learning Hebrew as a religious act.

Boy, I am tired. The energy has risen as far as my hand — so I can write. But it hasn't yet got to my head, so I write only no-header things. I was going to Yad Vashem, the holocaust museum, this morning. The bus leaves on the hour — that's why I went into the museum, because I had 40 minutes until the bus. I dropped into 4000 years of cleverly told history.

Oh, I noticed the paper placemat has something in unrecognizable script — must be Armenian. It doesn't look like Cyrillic characters. Must be the name of this place, which is Armenian Tavern.

It is almost 2:30 — at 4:30 I go to the YMCA to see a class in Hebrew which I may join. I shall first go back to Beit Shmuel to lie down a while. I must remember how to say 205 in Hebrew to the desk clerk. After they told me half a dozen times, I think I have it. Mataiim ve hamesh — is that it? Think so. Hebrew often has single, pair and plural, instead of just single and plural. So 200 is not formed like 300 or 400, etc.. Hundreds is "meod" I think — so 300 would be something like "slosha meod" — but 200 is "mataiim".

❧ *14* ❧
Yad Vashem

What is this dark river that runs in us and can be harnessed to such things?

Jerusalem   Thursday, November 9, 9:08 AM
King David Street — the bus stop. Waiting. Number 18 or 21. Bright sun, bright sky, bright buildings.

9:09 AM   On the bus — it may be 21H. Where it goes, I go. Where I want to go is Yad Vashem — the holocaust museum. There goes a woman running in short shorts, in bright sun. Life in the city. She went around the corner of the cemetery. A corner I know well, having passed it many times. A young man sneezes, then crosses in front of the bus. We are going up the hill, toward Jaffa Gate. Palm trees in front of the city walls. We turn hard left. This is where I walked yesterday morning. This morning I didn't wake until 6:45, so I didn't walk. A big stomach man — suit, hat, tie — runs for the bus — a heart attack candidate. We may be on Jaffa Road. Hard to tell — a street looks different to a bus rider then it does to a walker. Ah — good woman — she asked the driver in English: Are you going to the Central Bus Station? — and he grunted — which I take as affirmative. One grunt is affirmative, two is negative — at least that is the way it is in English. The Central Bus Station is a known point — because I walked by it the other day, when returning from the Knesset.

Jaffa Road

The city seems gray-somber this bright day. Aftermath of assassination. At least I feel that way. A girl, her back straight and proud as ever can be, walks briskly in front of the bus. Oh — about 17, but no nonsense about her — she will rule the world. There is a crush of buses in front of us, all stopped. I count five. It is a sun sparkle day — after yesterday's rain swept the sky, washed the streets and buildings. It is the winter of our time. People wear jackets and sweaters. Now we go by small shops of old Jaffa Road, of old-new Jerusalem. Is this the Central Bus Station? Most everyone gets off. Old stone buildings —

one story — line this road. When they were built the road was dirt and camels. Maybe. The sunlight is astounding — a call to life. My throat tells a different story — the air looks crystal pure, but has an acrid smell and sting. Here we are, next to the building where I drank grapefruit juice on Monday. A young man gets on, the fringes of his prayer shawl trail behind his leather jacket. Now the bus is at the furthest reach of the known world — beyond here I have not walked.

This bus driver talks. In a mile or so I will mention to him my destination. But I think Yad Vashem is on the outskirts of the city, so I have a ways to go. A tall young man walks by, his long neck comes from his collar at a forward angle. He seems to be searching, seeking, not finding — a tall bird looking for sustenance.

The two signals I get confuse me — my eyes see the clarity of morning sun and air, my lungs receive the acid sting. I stand, lean over — Yad Vashem? I say to the driver. He pauses, flicks his hand, three fingers go up. Three stations, he says.   He looks like a tank commander. I have confidence.

9:43 AM   Off the bus, a parking lot, tour buses. I follow the people, they go up a gravel walk, through a rose garden, up a hill. Are they going to Rabin's grave? I see no signs. The path is soon bordered by pine trees. Metal plaques. I look at one. Hebrew and Roman characters. President of the German something. I come to a wide stone-paved plaza. To the right is a dark marble square, flowers and wreathes. Is this Rabin's grave? Only one man goes off toward it — I follow him. On the marble side is engraved הרצל Herzl — it is the grave of Herzl. I go on a bit — here is a large metal sign, a bit worn and let go —

in Hebrew and English: "Mount Herzl — National Site of the State of Israel and the Jewish People. Here is the tomb of Theodore (Binyamin Zeev) Herzl (1860 – 1904), the founder of the Zionist movement and the visionary of the Jewish State."

10:05 AM   Yes, the people are going to the grave of Yitzhak Rabin. A hundred people stand in a loose circle about the grave. Silent. The grave is heaped four feet high with wreathes and surrounded by hundreds of small burning candles. I stand silently a few minutes.

10:10 AM   I walk a little ways from Rabin's grave. Here are many neat graves in stone-fenced plots with headstones in Hebrew. I can make out בן on each one, which means "son", and also "of the age of". The ages are 19, 21, 23, 26 — the oldest I see in two rows is 33. These are the military graves. A small dark woman puts flowers in a jar on one grave.   Ai ai, what a world, what a place.

10:32 AM   I come down the hill. The stone building at the street is the Herzl museum. I start up the sidewalk. Puzzled. I ask a school girl: Where is Yad Vashem? Here, she points to a road alongside the Herzl museum, walk down there, you will see it.

10:56 AM   I sit on a bench in the shade of the trees at the end of the Avenue of the Righteous Gentiles.

12:22 PM   I sit on a rock wall in the statuary garden, behind the museum. I am numb and tired.

12:51 PM   I walk in this place called The Valley of the Communities. Huge canyons created by great blocks of yellow-tan Jerusalem stone. And on polished stone surfaces 20 feet high, set in the stone canyons, are carved the names of the villages and towns, the communities destroyed. I found the stone surface called Bialystok, for my father came from that region. And on the stone surface, seventh from the top, is KRYNKI קרינקי — my father's town.

Valley of the Communities at Yad Vashem

2:04 PM   I eat. In the cafeteria of Yad Vashem. I am very hungry. The room is bright — I sit under a skylight and beside banks of blossoming impatiens, pink, orange, white, rose, purple, fuchsia. There is the bright chatter of the others in the room. My mind removes itself, reserves itself, comes to the bright food, the bright flowers, the bright sound. But my body is still in nervous rattle, tight and frightened. I don't understand Nazis. I don't understand people who do that to others. Why? Why in Bosnia now? What is this dark river that runs in us and can be harnessed to such things?

2:21 PM I finish eating. I sit here at the table picking my teeth. I am still in a nervous jangle. I look at the xeroxed map of Yad Vashem. I'll go to the other places the woman circled for me — the Children's Memorial, the Hall of Remembrance, the Hall of Names. — As I walk from the cafeteria, I see that on a small table near the entrance there is a color photo of Rabin and a small vase of flowers.

3:20 PM Back on #21 bus, back to the central city. Good guy driver — he opens the door to whoever waves, where they are — doesn't make them run to spot X. On the street, the passengers board from long traffic islands.

3:54 PM A place note. This is the same chair, same table. Same café. What is it — TOLT SHIMSHUM? — something like that. Ah, here is the name in Hebrew on the little menu card. תמול שלשום — so, from that, we make it TMOL SHLSHOM. So be it. Herb tea. That's all!? said the waitress.

So — I will look over the Hebrew textbook I just bought. It is for the Y class. Did I mention the Y class? I went there yesterday afternoon — to the easy one, at 4:30. But I intended to also stay for the more advanced one — at 7:30. Not to be — I have to struggle to reach the level of the 4:30 class — who have been doing an hour and a half twice a week since mid-September.

4:11 PM A strange thing — I sit hunched over my book. A woman speaks right into my ear. No one near me. It is the young woman at the next table. She is ten feet away, but she sits with her back to an arch which, on its other side, comes down right behind me. So her voice came right into my ear.

5:16 PM   The interesting thing is that I feel so at ease in this place. Why? I like the books, the ambience, the quiet people, the quiet music. Something else? Is it that this is a gay-friendly place? There isn't anything obviously gay about the place. The clientele don't look gay. Some of the bookmarks posted on the wall near me are from feminist bookstores in the US, there is a small notice on the small board near the door advising of the meeting of a gay/lesbian group, some man has a notice for a male squash partner, which might mean more.   But I think it is mostly that this is a very civilized, cultured place — decent people being decent to one another. No other place in Israel have I felt as comfortable — not that I have felt terribly uncomfortable here in Israel.

I hear a siren somewhere not close. Which reminds me of another favorable feature — this place is not on a street with autos.

5:43 PM   I hear the young man speaking — an American voice, I hear other American voices. These are Americans — very American. Are they Jews? Probably. Is that how the German Jews felt in 1933? Very German? How long had Jews been in Germany? A thousand years? And had begun being emancipated, entering mainstream German society after the French revolution, 1789. I read that book by Hannah Arendt about the German Jewish woman who held the famous salon in Berlin around 1800, frequented by the Prussian nobility. And Heinrich Heine? Mendelssohn — his father converted to Christianity. Jews in the German army in World War I. Along comes Hitler and this incredible brutality. How? Why? Where did it come from? This mad hatred. Is it Christianity? The teaching of the Christian church? Naziism was only the most recent manifestation. The brutal Russians, the pograms, the killings and expulsions over the centuries from the countries of Western Europe, Spain, the Inquisition. What horror. Israel is a response to all that. And that religious adherence to the land. That teaching of the Torah — going through it once every year, marked on the body, circumcision. That fierce, unextinguishable attachment to peoplehood, the continuing community. No other people so fierce an attachment. Why? What is it? That is what I want to explore.

Jerusalem: a wall and a shadow

❦ *15* ❧
Israel Museum

Thanks for talking American to us

Jerusalem   **Friday, November 10, 10:12 AM**
In the rain, with the kids. Waiting for the bus. Number
9 — to the Israel Museum. Everyone crowds under the
narrow bus shelter. As in California: dry country people
abhor getting rained on. I am fortunate to have a seat
in the shelter. The stream runs in the gutter, full a foot
wide and a couple inches deep. And the autos splash by. I
was bent on walking to the museum because I didn't see
the #9 listed on the bus stops I passed on Karen Hayosod
St. I took out my map on a rainy corner. An old man came
up.   Eh, eh, he said.   Do you speak English? I asked.
Which way to the Israel Museum?   The number 9 bus,
he said, come, come.   So I followed him, at his shuffle
along, for two blocks. My goodness, all the buses passing
are tour buses. And the chattering kids get wet.

10:23 AM   On the #9. Barely. The closing doors barely
admitted my rear. But I have a seat right behind the
driver. I stepped over a burly fellow wearing a kippa to
get to this window seat.   And he said Yafe (Beautiful).
Then he said something else in Hebrew and I said Ani lo

mdaber Ivrit. Ah, he said. Museo, I said. Ah, he said. And soon left. A kid sat next to me, spoke English, told me where to get off the bus.

Now — 10:38, I sit on a padded bench in the museum entrance.

10:46 AM Now in the museum proper. Earlier, when I came up to the ticket booth, there were four elderly Americans. How much is that in dollars? one asked. Apparently the clerk couldn't tell them. A young man in line said — Seven dollars. They paid, one of the ladies turned to me — We aren't crowding in front of you, she said, we came in the wrong way. Then, at the information desk, I stood behind them again. There is a guided tour in English at 11, said the information man, and then, at 12:30, a guided tour of the Shrine of the Book. "That's what we're here for," said the only man of the group, gruffly, emphatically — I received it as: "This is why we came to Jerusalem, because of the Bible, we aren't Jews, we are not concerned about your new-fangled country and all its old-fangled problems." As they left the information desk, one woman said "Thanks for talking American to us" to the information man who spoke with a slight British accent.

2:50 PM. Smoke. That is the worst thing. Lots of cigarette smoke. But I don't know what else is open. When I stumbled upon this place a few days ago, she said they serve ham sandwiches, so I knew they wouldn't close early for the Shabbat, as the vegetarian restaurant did. We would lose our kashrut (the certification that they follow Jewish dietary rules), the kid at the veggie place said. I bought a chunk of cauliflower pie as insurance — to take out. They wouldn't let me sit down.

So. After the smoke, it's wet feet. I walked a mile in pouring-down rain. Yes, I had my brilliant blue gortex jacket, yes, the wool tweed hat, yes, my fold-up umbrella. But my shoes are soaked, my pants wet.

I am not even going to think about the room at Beit Shmuel. This is the day I don't have reserved. I asked yesterday. The woman at the desk said, Ask us in the morning. I asked in the morning — she still wasn't certain. I said I'd call at noon. I didn't. I was at the museum and walking in the rain. Now I drink the beer, wait for the chicken. Feel nervous energy bubble in me. Can I be quieter, calmer? I stop writing for a moment, fold my hands, breathe in.   I simmer down a little. The fellow is not smoking anymore. I was tired when I left the museum. Museum tired — which is in the kidneys, the small of the back. Waited for the bus, wasn't certain #17 would go close to Ben Yehuda St. and the veggie restaurant. Started walking. A pleasant walk, through the park in the valley leading on from the museum and the Knesset building. But then the rain, first just drops, then patter, then hard and rivulets driving down from the side streets, rushing down stone stairways.

Oh my, now the music is unpleasant. Pow pow pow. I hate it. This place is called סטודין — which is Studin. I pour another glass of beer. Maybe I'll become stinking drunk. Not possible. My — my meal is taking a long time. Maybe they are doing it from scratch. Vegetable soup and chicken with sesame.   After the veggie restaurant — Ah, the soup — very hot.   After the veggie restaurant, I went to Café Tmol Shilshom. I thought they would still be serving because they have poetry readings on Friday evening.   Alas, I opened the door — the room had been charged with chairs, an audience was already listening to a reading. No food there.

Now — things are better. The hot soup goes to my stomach, battles with the wet shoes for the feet. All the other patrons have left, the air is all mine. Two new kids come in. I have at least 40 years on everyone else I've seen in this café (קפה). The placemat also says קפה ליד הגלריה. The first word I see as café, the second "lid" — Oh — the chicken. Ai — shades of the Colonel. Big mound of fried chicken on a platter of cucumber and tomato slices. Six months maximum daily allowance of fat, saturated fat, and cholesterol. No wonder all the other patrons are under 25 — you don't live past 34 on this. But tasty. Jerusalem fried chicken.

I think back to last Sunday, when I sat on the terrace of the Quarter Café, in the Old City. A woman at the next table was saying that in Italy they don't call it Jerusalem artichoke, they call it Jewish artichoke.   Strange day, last Sunday, when I was one of the few in Jerusalem who didn't know what had happened. I noticed nothing strange in the demeanor of people all through the day. Except. Except, when I first entered Jaffa Gate, I went to the Tourist Information Office just inside the gate. I asked the woman there for a map of the city. She gave me a look, which I took as something like Why are you bothering me with this now? She was signaling that something was very wrong, but I didn't pick it up.   Now I am cutting the fattened breading off the chunks of chicken before I eat them.

It is now 3:52 — in a half hour it will be getting dark. Will I find a little market open? I didn't worry about this last Friday because then I was leading the religious life. Wailing at the Wall, being fed later — I guess the food was prepared earlier in the day. I should pay and get along — to see whether I still have a room at Beit Shmuel, for one thing. But the waitress in talking on the telephone.

6:24 PM   When I came back to Beit Shmuel a couple hours ago I found I still had my room for tonight. So. I sit in my room. Discontent. A little. I don't want to walk back into the Ben Yehuda area — it is wet and cold outside and everything is probably closed. I went around the corner a few minutes ago to see if there was a service at the Hebrew Union College. There wasn't.

∼ *16* ∽
Arab East Jerusalem

Same people, same anxieties, same joys?

Jerusalem   **Saturday, November 11, 12:06 PM**
Sitting in the courtyard of the Rockefeller Museum,
in east Jerusalem. A stone and water place — the
courtyard. I came to this museum about 10:30. I walked
through the Arab quarter of the Old City and along a
boulevard outside the walls. This area is very different
from the Jewish new city to the west. Israelis seem
almost totally absent. There are Arabs and a sprinkling
of tourists. The Rockefeller Museum is of a different
time than the Israel Museum I saw yesterday. It is of the
British Mandate period, the collections are interesting
but poorly displayed and labeled.   I look up at the
smooth stone wall of this courtyard in front of me. It is
pocked by small shallow exploded-out spots. Rifle fire?

12:22 PM   I have left the museum building. I sit on a
low stone wall in the courtyard in front of the entrance.
Behind me there is a terrace with two rows of olive trees,
behind that and below, the road, and across the road
the north wall of the Old City. Through the olive trees
I see the slope of what I think is the Mount of Olives.

Courtyard at Rockefeller Museum

Carrying on with my non-Jewish Shabbat, I think I will walk along the wall to Notre Dame, the Catholic hospice, which the guide book says serves very good meals.

12:57 PM   Way out, far out, in the bosom. Of the church — culinary division. I asked to look at a menu when I entered. La Rotisserie, this place. My goodness, incredibly cheap for such an elegant looking place. Now I look at the menu again.   I didn't notice. The $ at the top of the price columns.   Priced in dollars, not shekels, so multiply by three.

So — there I was in the Rockefeller Museum. The curled skeleton in the case. 10,000 BCE. The ivory board game. 1800 BCE? 1200? I forget. Maybe it wasn't even marked. No better, no worse, no different. From me and you.

Like learning a language. When you don't understand, it sounds mysterious, important, portentous. When you can understand, it is ordinary things being said. 10,000 years ago, 4000 years ago, same people, same anxieties, same joys? Or can you say the same dimensions — most banal or everyday and some reaching for something, imagining something?

This is quite a dignified place — La Rotisserie. Yellow Jerusalem stone blocks make the walls, marble the floors, Roman arches, Oriental carpets. I sit in something of a forecourt — kind of outside the wall, but enclosed, roofed. The only other diners in this room now are two men in dark suits, speaking — no, not French, not German, not Italian. I don't know — Rumanian? They speak together softly, confidentially. Maybe it is Italian, I hear quando, si, si. Maybe a dialect.

1:44 PM   I have finished the fish, et al. I sip the rest of the wine in my glass, chew at a breadstick. I have been feeling a little down and dopey today. Being alone, not talking much, having no close contact. This morning when I came down to breakfast at Beit Shmuel, the dining room was running over with people. I sat down at a table and soon was surrounded by a group of Britishers, connected, chatting, having done that, going to do this, and so and so went to a nightclub last night, asked to borrow my white sweater. The couple across from me bowed their heads in silence a few moments before starting to eat. Did he have something in his bag he wanted? she asked. The book to read on the flight? They were perfectly familiar, click clack, edge to edge, corner to corner.

Ah. Minor success. The waiter said: You wish something

else? Tea, I said. You want mint — fresh mint — in it?
Yes, I said — matter of fact, put in lots of mint and don't
put in tea.

Maybe I should do something risky. Like go to Cairo.
That's what I thought when I saw the Egyptian artifacts
at the Rockefeller. Ah, the mint tea — and he brings a
little plate with two stuffed dates. My time in Jerusalem
has been somewhat out of joint since my study program
came apart. Although I am still studying Hebrew. I
bought the book for the class at the YMCA and I will go
there again on Monday and Wednesday afternoons.

What have I done in Jerusalem? I arrived a week ago
Thursday. Thursday afternoon getting into a hotel, in
the evening my first session with David. I was a Talmud
student all the way through Sunday, Wailing at the Wall
Friday and Saturday. Monday, I participated, as I could,
in Rabin's funeral. Tuesday, this and that and discovered
Tmol Shilshom. Wednesday, the Jerusalem museum at
Tower of David. Thursday, Yad Vashem; yesterday the
Israel Museum; today the Rockefeller.

6:14 PM   I have to say where I am, what I am doing.
Because he said: Hey John, you have your water from
the Jordan? I am sitting before a table in the lobby of the
YMCA. A group of 30-ish people — oh, about eight of
them, men and women, sit at the next table, chattering,
anxious, about to jump. Jump to somewhere — an
airport, a bus, a far city, another life. I have been sitting
here for about 20 minutes, reading through previous
pages of this. And they have been next to me, putting out
that intensity, that excitement. Leaving Jordan, crossing
Jordan. And I am just sitting at the table. Now one of
them begins tapping away at a small drum, adding

another sound of nervous intensity. Is that good or bad? That nervous intensity? Would it be good for me if I had it? Would it be good for the Jews? — just noodling. Maybe it comes from lack of sleep. It is not good. I don't want it. There — the fellow starts on the drum again. I feel my fingers tighten on the pen as I write. Now they have all left, but I still hear the drum. Drums in the night. Voices and drums. Save us, save me, from voices and drums. What will he do with the water of the Jordan? I don't mock; I don't know. There are purposes for water. The mind goes round in water, makes things of water. Water, rain, snow, dew, steam, blood, water water water. Mayim mayim mayim מים.

6:59 PM   Still at the Y, still at the table. Two men talk amiably in Hebrew behind me. I pick up words. Ma omer? — What are you saying? Ani — I. Hebrew seems to be a clearly spoken language. It doesn't slur away, like French or American English. I yawn. It seems late although it is just turning 7. The night begins early; by 4:30 the daylight is already fading. And it becomes tomorrow — for the Jewish day begins at sunset. Thus, the Shabbat is over already.   Amazing thing, this revival of Hebrew. I think the guide in the Shrine of the Book yesterday said that Israeli school kids can read the Essene scrolls. I am not sure she said that because the Shrine of the Book was the Scream of the Loon yesterday afternoon: people everywhere, voices echoing and obliterating one another. I left the group midway through. The Israel Museum itself had a lovely guided tour.

Ele so and so, Ele so and so, Ele so and so, says the speaker behind me. "Ele" means "These". So. I think I'll have a make-do supper tonight. This afternoon I bought from a street vendor in Arab Jerusalem two apples and two persimmons. I already ate one of each. I shall eat the other two and call it supper.   Col ha yehudim — All the Jews, says the man in back of me. They must be talking politics.

7:19 PM   I folded my tent in the lobby and started to walk out. I saw, on an easel, a painting and a sign "Exposition in the lobby" — so I went around the room and looked at them. An old man in a black suit sat in a chair, against the wall. He was one of the animated talkers who sat behind me in the lobby. His partner has left. I think they both work here.

Nice waitress — she came back to tell me, in difficult English, that the Moroccan soup doesn't have meat in it but is made from a meat stock. Because that is where I am. Not quite a restaurant — that is in the next, the noisy, room, with the white tablecloths. Here the tables are bare grey marble — been here since — oh — 1924 — I'd say. Yes, this is across from the lobby of the Y. A pleasant place.   I look behind me. There is that interesting old gentleman I saw when I was walking to Beit Shmuel about 3 PM. He wears a black Indian turban, has a white British Army mustache — say about 1875. Tall, distinguished.

The lady at the near table asked about the Moroccan soup also. She said, Oh no, I don't eat meat. The waitress comes with my soup and my bottled water. The paper napkin says "Le Tsriff — since 1978". They must, then, have gotten the 1924 tables at auction.   This soup is too meaty for me. I have lost my taste for meaty. I like the quiet tastes. Tastes without blood.

This place has a peculiar name. Le seems French, but

Tsriff seems Hebrew. As a matter of fact, the name is given in Hebrew on the napkin as הצריף — which is Ha Tsriff — the Ha is the Le.

Now, here is the Moroccan salad — I am doing all Moroccan. It is red peppers — I think braised — like Celso does it in Madrid. The waitress said, in her inexact English, that it was burnt. Maybe — I think it is sort of burnt and the skin is peeled off. There is a cooking term I can't think of: braised blanched, bruxilated. Something. I notice that the wall beside me is carpeted. Doesn't go well with the marble tables, but it probably keeps the room quiet.

❧ 17 ❧

Complicated Place, Jerusalem

47 Narkis Street — that's it, for sure

Jerusalem   Sunday, November 12, 11:45 AM
Well, this is an interesting adventure. Pepin asked
me to look up this man in Jerusalem who is to speak
at a conference in Madrid in December: "The Second
European Conference on Is Intelligence Modifiable?"
Good question, no? The opening address will be by
Professor Reuven Feuerstein of Jerusalem.

But first I should introduce myself. I am the one sitting
on the small sidewalk terrace of Pera e Mela, an Italian
dairy restaurant on Narkis Street. The napkin says
"אגס ותפוח Poire et Pomme". So now we know what Mela
means in Italian. And also the two Hebrew words. But
not how to pronounce the Hebrew words.

The program for the December conference gives the title
of Prof. Feuerstein's address as: "Modifying Intelligence
at the End of the 20th Century: Liberal Fantasy or
Scientific Reality?" Prof. Feuerstein is the honorary
president of EAMC which, give or take a few initials, is
the European Association for Mediated Learning and

Cognitive Modifiability. It is the EAMC's conference.

Pepin is keenly interested in whether it is possible to recover the ability to think (brain function) lost through heroin use. He sent a letter to me in Netanya asking that I look up Prof. Feuerstein and gave me his address: 47 Narkis Street. So that is one of the things I set out to do this morning. I now have a real street map of Jerusalem, not one of those inadequate tourist maps. I found Mordichai Narkis Street on the map, running off King George Avenue, on the other side of Independence Park from Beit Shmuel and not far from where Ben Yehuda and Hillel cross King George.

I went to the bank on Hillel Street, then went to the copy shop, also on Hillel — but the machine was being repaired by two fellows, and the operator, who did such a nice job for me last Tuesday, sat idle. He spread his hands, palms up.   When will it be fixed? I asked.   But he didn't understand. I pointed at my watch. He looked at his watch, said something — I think "shtiem", which means either 2 o'clock or in two hours — it was then 10:30.

So I went in search of Prof. Feuerstein. I walked several blocks down King George — no Narkis. I asked — the fellow said, Go right here and keep going right. I came to a corner with no street signs. Half-block away, I saw this restaurant. I entered, the woman didn't speak English. I said Rechov Narkis?   Po, po, she said — Here, here. So I began looking for number 47. The first building was marked 2, so #47 was a good way along, on a steep downhill. I walked about three blocks, saw #39 — the street then was at the bottom of the hill and turned sharply to the right. There was a two-story, block-long building — looked like a school. A young man sat in front on a chair set in the sunlight of the sidewalk. I asked him. No, he said, this is Lod Street.

I walked back to #39. I saw there was one more, last, house next to it, #41. The iron gate was not locked. I walked to the front door and buzzed — this is a more formidable task than in an American neighborhood — the houses here have stone walls about them, a bit of a fortress-like aspect. No one home. I walked downhill again. Across the street several people were standing talking beside a gate — three middle-aged people and a young man in the full yeshiva costume: black coat, black hat. Do you speak English? I asked. Of course — Americans. But they didn't even know where Narkis Street was.   Where you from? The older fellow asked. California, I said.   I have a daughter in Los Angeles, he said, I'll walk with you. So we walked across the street as a taxi stopped to make a turn. I asked the driver. Go further that way, he said, and pointed to the street he came from, which started where Narkis turned to Lod and doubled back below the hill Narkis came down.

I know that first building is of the telephone company, said my friend from across the street. I went into the telephone building, which had a glassed-in information desk in the entryway. Do you speak English? I asked the fellow (beard and kippa). "Of course" — another American. Here, he said, I'll show you, and we went out to the sidewalk. You see that tall building coming out down there. Yes. That's it, he said, the Institute. I'll try it, I said. No, he said, that's it — for sure.

So I walked down to an impressive building of smooth-cut yellow Jerusalem stone. Just as I came to the front doors (with the brass letters overhead that said Institute for Developmental Learning — or something like that) the doors swung open and some dozen well-dressed people came out into the courtyard. I went in and introduced myself to a man in the lobby, told him my Spanish friends worked with ex-drug addicts, were investigating the effect of heroin on brain function, had asked me to obtain literature and invite Professor Feuerstein to visit them when he was in Spain. You can ask him for yourself, he is out there — pointing to the group in the courtyard. He is the one in the black suit.

Prof. Feuerstein was a short man, white hair, long white beard, black suit and black beret. I told him my story. Come with me, he said. We eventually took the elevator three stories up to his office, but he stopped on the way four or five times to speak to people. The building was new and beautiful — and the work seems to be with retarded kids. When we got to his office, Prof. Feuerstein said, And what do you do? I work as a lawyer, I said. Oh, he said, raising both hands — as if to say, who knows what to do with lawyers? He turned me over to his secretary, who gathered for me a thick pile of pamphlets and reprints.

So — then I came back up to this restaurant. Where I have eaten well while scribbling the above. Now — 1:17 PM — I must move on, for I am sitting outside and the blood cools sitting outside on a November day in Jerusalem. I think — what a different world this is from where I was yesterday — in Arab East Jerusalem. Oh my; Oy vey.

1:30 PM Here I am again at the copy shop. A warmer place — and only two blocks away from the restaurant. I so much prefer scraping away the day doing this sort of thing then going on a tourist jaunt. It is much easier, for one thing, to schmooze about than to be a tourist. It is not often recognized that being a hell-for-leather, show-me-all-the-sights tourist is very hard work. I sit on the couch near the coffee machine, hand pages 13 to 33 to the nice fellow, who understands no English. I turn my hand up and down — meaning both sides, and then spread all five fingers — meaning five copies. I also say hamesh, five. And a girl picks it up, says it to him.   So I think it will all be done right. He did it perfectly last time.

On the way here, I walked a block along King George Street. Little shops — very modish women's clothing, a silversmith, Chinese herb shop, a design belt shop — "design your own belt" — super sophisticated — how will it mesh with East Jerusalem? Or with Mea Sherim, the super-Orthodox neighborhood a mile away? Complicated place, Jerusalem.

Oh — when I went inside the Italian restaurant to pay, I noticed they had a color photo of Rabin, framed, on the wall, with a legend in Hebrew underneath it. I also noticed in the lobby of Prof. Feuerstein's Institute, there was a framed color photo of Rabin with several articles and legends surrounding it. In death, he is someone very important here. There is an "Avraham Lincoln" street that runs off Rechov David Ha-melech (King David Street), at the side of the YMCA. Rabin may take on that sort of meaning in the story of this country. A man who saw the worst of war and came to the goal of peace and reconciliation — and was killed for it.

How do the assassinations balance? The advocates for peace killed as against the advocates for war killed? My guess is that it is much more dangerous for a leader to advocate peace than to advocate war.

Yasser Arafat, Shimon Peres and Yitzhak Rabin receiving the 1994 Nobel Peace Prize "for their efforts to create peace in the Middle East".

1:57 PM Oh, oh — he is having trouble with the machine. I think he wants to run the pages automatically, instead of hand placing each sheet as he did the last time.

3:30 PM Waiting. In line at the main post office on Jaffa Road.

6 PM Beit Shmuel — upstairs in the auditorium. An event — a panel discussion of the three monotheistic religions. I didn't even know there was this auditorium. Very nicely appointed, comfortable. There is in Israel much of this modern, comfortable place and ambience.

I kind of think of it as Best American — as opposed to McDonalds, TV serials, pop music. The speaker begins. In Hebrew — Ai, I hope some of the panel will speak English.

8:25 PM   It was almost all in Hebrew — except for the Sister who spoke on Christianity — she spoke English. But I sat through the whole thing — good practice just to listen even if I understand only occasional words.

~ *18* ~

Blood, Stones and Roses

The workmen are Muslims

Jerusalem   Monday, November 13, 7:26 AM
Up, showered, dressed. Bright morning. Probably chilly. I
shall put on a sweater, walk the half block to King David
Street (Rechov David Ha-melech) and buy *The Jerusalem
Post*, then to breakfast downstairs.

8:26 AM   Late breakfast. I bought the paper and kept
on going. The morning said "Walk". I'll eat breakfast
out, I thought, maybe at Café Tmol Shilshom.   Before
arriving there, I passed a dairy restaurant — upstairs.
I went up — no, still closed. So was Café Tmol.   I kept
walking — Jaffa Rd. and beyond — a good mile or two.
Then I returned to Beit Shmuel and here I am, among
the late wakers, the last of the breakfasters.

10:44 AM   I walked to the south of Beit Shmuel, toward
the old-new neighborhood founded by Moses Montifiore
in — what? — the 1870s? This is to the east, toward the
Old City, from the big square block of the King David
Hotel. This area was no-man's land from 1949 to 1967.
Now, where I am (not yet in the Montifiore neighborhood,

which is a pretty expanse of yellow-stone houses, yellow-stone walks, artisans and restaurants), there is a grassy park which faces the wall of the Old City across the valley. A valley, I am sure, known and renowned, but I forget its name.

I sit on a big rock alongside a gravel path in the shade of a — no, it is not an olive tree, although the leaves are olive green. They are long graceful leaves, reaching, playing, splaying, swaying in the air. I look at those old walls across the renowned valley. I feel antipathy toward the stone walls, the narrow lanes, the crowded stone houses of the Old City. What have these old stones that can compare with one branch of this tree above me, or the beautiful live blush of the roses further down this gravel path? Those old stones are so snared in blood, cruelty, destruction and construction. It is tiring, so many thousands of years of compounded stupidity. The stone walls turn me aside.

But — what of all my feeling for the on-going community, for the sharing from century to century, millennium to millennium? For the immensely clever people who found how to make from stone something that cuts, how to gather food and store it, how to melt and re-melt rocks to make all sorts of useful metal tools. And people who thought and tried their best, helped one another, wrote their yearning and insight? All that stuff — for it is progressive — we have gathered control, ability to live more comfortably. The people in the walls did that — besides building and wrecking, building and wrecking. Well, I don't know. I sit on the pinnacle of comfort. I have time enough, comfort enough, to be discontent. What am I if I don't connect with everything that has gone before?

Well, what is the tree that shades me, what are the roses?   I shall go on to Montifiore's neighborhood — is it called Yemin Moshe? Yes, says the map. I'll go on to see if there is a café where I can sit and do the homework for my Hebrew class at the Y, which is at 4:30 this afternoon.

11:40 AM   I wander. Asked a girl sitting on a stairway of Yemin Moshe: Is there a café?   Over there, she pointed.   No, this is a restaurant, said the man sitting at the bar, over there, across the bridge, there are many cafés. I went on. Was this the bridge? — it was more of a road causeway crossing the valley. I went down to it, crossed it, walked down the grass slope of the valley to a large stone building. The brass letters on the stone said Alpert Music Center (no relation). But no café. I saw a pedestrian bridge high above, climbed stone steps up — I was back on the busy roadway that came from the causeway. Yes, here is a terrace with tables, overlooking the valley, the Alpert Center. But the autos go by. The charm of Yemin Moshe is that there are no autos, noise, acrid smell. But — here I sit, with orange juice and tea, the sunlight on the back of my neck, the people behind me speaking French, not a word of which I understand. To my homework.

12:19 PM   I read a page of Hebrew; many words I do not understand. I shall look for them in my Hebrew-English dictionary, which is in my room.   On the roadway the autos go by, go by, go by. Do they go somewhere or do they only go by?   Across the valley there is another road coming down to the causeway and then going up again to Jaffa Gate of the Old City.   Below me there is a tree — its top comes about level with my eyes. It has lost many of its leaves. The leaves look something like a peach tree's. Many birds fly to the tree, rest a moment,

fly on. There goes one bird — almost straight up. Up up
and then he turns and dives straight down. They are tiny
birds, about four inches long, brown and black striped
backs, gray underneath. Now a bus-load of Germans has
settled here on the terrace.

12:42 PM   I walk away from my terrace, cross the
curved pedestrian bridge. Here is a new stone wall,
stone steps. I go up the steps. A park. A large plaza with
a monumental fountain — in the center an enormous
bronze figure of intricate curves and swirls, around the
perimeter, many life-sized, stylized, bronze lions. The
stonework around the fountain is not finished. Two
workmen sit, eating lunch. On a bench, another man
stands, barefoot. When I first see him, he is so still I
think maybe it is a statue. But no, he bends, then kneels
with his forehead on the bench. He is praying, I realize.
The workmen are Muslims.

A park, a fountain — bronze lions

~ *19* ~

Feeling Squinched

Perhaps I must put myself in water

Still Monday, 1:18 PM   I wandered around — until I finally found — the YMCA. Here I am, outside, at a linen-covered table. First I went to the restaurant in Yemin Moshe. Asked to look at a menu. Expensive and the waiter wore a tuxedo. No, no — so I walked through Yemen Moshe — and — I was back near Beit Shmuel. I realized I must eat and finish my homework by 4:30. So — to Beit Shmuel —   but they don't serve lunch. Upstairs? I asked. (There is a mysterious complex upstairs, which I only discovered last night.) The woman at the desk didn't know. I went out and up the stairs. Yes, they serve lunch, but it was over. Until what time do you serve? I asked.   One, half past one, she said. (It was 1:10 then).   Anyway, I went out through the Hebrew Union — it seems Beit Shmuel is in the same complex as the Hebrew Union, although they front on different streets a block apart.

Umm — this meal at the Y is surprisingly good. To start — separate little dishes of eggplant, zucchini and dried tomatoes — and sour cream. And the setting is pleasant

— behind the tall cypresses of the courtyard, far from the street noise. Looming beyond the cypresses is the great square bulk of the King David Hotel across the street.

The Jerusalem YMCA

Against the pale yellow stone of the King David, I see the sun setting on the British Empire.   My spinach pie arrives. First class, old boy, first class.   What are we to think of the British Empire?   Ah, here are the birds again. These are bigger. Flitting about, standing on nearby chairs, eyeing my spinach pie. Simple minds, simple needs. Birds don't have empires, stock markets, or stone walls.   Compare a bird to the British Empire. First of all, we don't capitalize bird, while we do capitalize British Empire. Why? Because there are many birds but only one British Empire.   Second, the Empire had ranks and privileges, whereas the birds have pecking order.

6:21 PM   At Café Tmol Shimshol. I am not sure I got it right — the Tmol I have but — no it is Shilshom? That is how sounds come and go.   I have a slight headache. From putting on and taking off my strong glasses in the Hebrew class. Boy — Money. I am — or am becoming — peculiar about money. I told the teacher at the end of the class that I hadn't paid yet and I would be at one more class. She said, Well you must pay for a month and that is 140 shekels and I must have a receipt at the next class.

I felt unhappy — that I was being overcharged. I went to the desk and said I wanted to pay. And the girl said, We need a note from your teacher saying how much. I said, She said 140 — but then I wasn't sure. 150? 140? So I left and felt messy in my mind. Now that I have talked to myself a little it seems okay. It is I who have set it up so I can go to only three classes. What is 140 shekels? $50. $16 a class. I should pay it. Of course. My ego wants to be treated as one who values money, receives value, is not ripped off, is not foolish. That was an element also, I know, in quitting David, my Talmud sage. He was charging $50 an hour, which struck me as high, especially when he was hanging his laundry part of the time.

Oh, oh, I just spooned into my mouth the half slice of lemon floating in my split pea and mint soup. I had forgotten it, when I saw it again it was covered with soup and I thought, my. what is this — a slice of potato?

But with David the main thing was I didn't feel compatible.   Ah, a second chance — here is another half lemon slice — my short-term memory is not all gone. I still remember the first lemon slice.   Boy, this place is quite full tonight. Every table taken.   I still must do one more thing to be square with David. I have a book he loaned me and also a kippa (skullcap) he loaned me. I want to walk over to the Shlomo Center in the Old City and leave them for him. But they don't open until 8 PM. So I must walk over in the night, which I don't like to do. Maybe after I leave here, I'll go to my room, pick up the two things and walk over to Shlomo Center. I hope I can find it. It is not far from the Western Wall.

Ai ai — I tend to be a petty one, a squinched guy. Like one of those squinched paper things that spreads large when put into water. Maybe I never put myself in water.

7:15 PM   Oh my, a young fellow with the galloping whoopees has sat down at the next table. You know, knees jumping to some internal frenzied beat — and stataco hand taps on the table when he first sat down. He looks quite normal but his internal rhythms set my teeth on edge.

❧ *20* ❧

Looking for Pardes (Paradise)

Can it be found in Jerusalem?

Jerusalem   Tuesday, November 14, 6:17 AM
I shall go for a walk before breakfast — maybe to the Old
City.

9:35 AM   Waiting for the #7 bus — on King George
St. Breathing the acid air. What is it that gives this
acid to car exhaust here? I am going to visit the Pardes
Institute – which, I am told, is a liberal yeshiva — a place
at which I might be comfortable.

[**2017 note:** Yeshiva (ישיבה) means, literally, "sitting".
Wikipedia says this: Yeshiva is a Jewish institution that
focuses on the study of traditional religious texts,
primarily the Talmud and Torah. Study is usually done
through daily shiurim (lectures or classes) and in study
pairs called havrutas ("friendship" or "companionship")
Havruta-style learning is one of the unique features of
the yeshiva.]

The buses stop and go. Number 4. A woman gets off #4,
asks me a question in Hebrew. The elderly lady sitting

next to me fields the question. Obviously it is directions to someplace. A hotel? I hear the word malon, which I think is hotel. What catches me is that the old lady, after giving directions, stands and watches that the woman is going in the right direction, even walks clear of the bus shelter to see better. (And she walks with difficulty.) I am moved by her continuing concern in this small matter for someone she doesn't know. The woman has asked for her help, and they are now connected — she is responsible for the woman.   Across this wide street is one of Jerusalem's imposing hotels.

9:46 AM   On the bus. It stops at the rail station. I must be alert — not to pass my destination.

10:05 AM   Walking. Off the bus. Across the boulevard. I cross behind a fellow all in khaki, even to a khaki kippa (skullcap). His shirt is ripped in back, he has white paint on his trousers, over his shoulder, on a bandolier torn but knitted together, is a submachine gun. Casual force. Then I see a brand-new building on the corner — Bank Hapoalim. I go in, try to put money, via VISA, in my sick cousin's account. Can't do it, says the British-accent fellow at the foreign currency desk. The main branch woman told me a few days ago it was no problem. But I am happy to not have this fellow do it — I can imagine the money stranded in cyberspace by incompetent handling. So. Onward.

10:15 AM   I reach a cross street, which commences with a little urban park with benches in the sun. The people on the benches are speaking Russian.

10:20 AM   A nice welcome: I came down the street a bit and there is a sign in Hebrew on a fence. It also says in Roman characters "Pardes", so I open the gate, walk across the short space to the building. A little reception office. No one there. Three doors, all closed, off this room. Shall I knock? I hesitate, look back out the front door. Here is a young fellow. You speak English? I ask.   No, he shakes his head. Please, he says — indicating a chair. Coffee?   Lo, I say.   Tea? Chai?   Ken, I say.   He prepares tea, sets out two thick glasses, points to a little package of sugar.   Lo, I shake my head at the package. He puts tea bags in the glasses. Two? he asks.   Lo, I say.   He pours the hot water. Speak Russian? he asks. Lo, I say, French, Spanish.

10:38 AM   Now I sit, back down the street on the same little urban park bench.   So — we talked a little — he with a little English, I with a little Hebrew. Very nice kid. I said, Pardes? This is the office?   He said Yes.   Ani rotze informatzia, I said — I want information — al Pardes, about Pardes.   He made a call. He will talk, he said, the director. A few minutes later the phone rang. The boy talked a while. Adon achad — one man — English — then he gave the phone to me. The director spoke English. You are in the wrong place, he said. The Pardes Institute has moved, it is at Pierre Koenig. Pierre? I said — like French?   Yes, he said, it is a French general — Koenig, like king.   Yes, I said — and wrote it at the bottom of this page.   Let me speak to the guard again, he said.   I gave the phone to the boy and drank the rest of my tea. When he hung up the phone, we shook hands. Toda raba, I said.   So — now I shall try the other Pardes. The director said, It is a big industrial building. The corner he gave me — he said it is at the corner of Rivka — is, I think, only a few blocks away.

11:19 AM   I have tried, God knows I have tried.

Now I stand at the entrance to the John F. Kennedy
Apprenticeship Center. I would like to sit on one of the
benches in front of the entrance, several feet away. But,
between me and the benches is an iron grill fence, eight
feet tall, and a locked gate. To keep the apprentices in?
Or, who?, out?   Ah, two men come to the other side of
the fence. Do you speak English? I say.   One seems
to nod Yes.   So I say, I look for the Pardes Institute.
They look baffled. They don't seem to understand
English.   Toda raba, I say, and they go back in the
building. I go back to the low wall at the entrance, and
begin to scribble again. A few minutes later one of the
men comes back to the fence. He moves his hands in front
of his chest, palms out toward me. What that? he says,
pointing to my writing folder and this sheet of paper.   I
am writing, I say.   Azur, he says, making the motion
again.   Can't write? I say, with a small smile.   Azur,
he says — which I know means forbidden in Hebrew.
Okay, I say, and I walk across the street, where I now
sit on a large rock. So — my goodness, I could write a
13-week TV thriller on my adventures this morning. I
walked the few blocks down to Pierre Koenig and Rivka. I
saw nothing that looked like a yeshiva.

11:35 AM   Now I have transferred a little ways to a
more comfortable place. A little falafel stand with some
plastic chairs and a plastic table in front. I pull one of the
white plastic chairs into the shade and sip from a can of
mango juice. I got mango because I know the word for
juice — mitz — but I don't know orange or grapefruit. So
she showed me mango and I said Ken, Ken.

To continue my story: I walked half a block down Pierre
Koenig. This is an area of warehouses and industrial
buildings mixed with apartment buildings. There are

on the ground floors some sort of discount furniture stores, and other stores. I went in one. No one to ask. Went in another, told a woman: I am looking for Pardes Institute. No, she said, I never heard of it, maybe it is on Rivka. I went back to the corner. At the corner, right at the corner, there is a vestige of olden times — a stone house with a ragged area at the side with some potted plants. Behind the house is a paved parking area. And behind the parking is an enormous four-story, block-long building, quite new. I walked up to this building. At an entrance I asked a man my two questions: 1. Do you speak English? and, 2. I am looking for the Pardes Institute. He never heard of it. I went inside. The inside of the first floor consists of a wide corridor with many pull-down iron shutters — the kind that protect shops on the street. Some of the shutters were rolled up and inside were what looked like small offices — desks, bookshelves, etc. I went in one and asked my two questions — this fellow was wearing a kippa so he was a religious type. He never heard of it. If it is in this building, it would be upstairs, he said.

Now it is 11:49 AM, and eight or ten students from the Kennedy Center have collected in front of the falafel stand. They look, curiously, at me scribbling.

So — I started up the stairs. Two young fellows — they looked like Arabs, started up behind me. I asked them my two questions. One fellow wore a black glove on his right hand. What is Pardes? he asked, a business? It is a yeshiva, I said. They looked puzzled. Toda raba (thank you), I said. Thank you, the fellow said, in English. Then, from above, a moment later, he called Welcome, you are welcome. I went out, found a bakery on the first floor, asked there. No, she didn't know. Went

out, looked at the Hebrew signs on the building to see if I
could spot anything that looked like Pardes פרדס. I saw
one sign that said פרדיין. I went up the stairs and
looked at it — it also said סילי — which I made out as
SILI - and then I saw it also said, in Roman characters,
SEALY — yes, mattresses. So — then I came back to the
corner — to the Kennedy Center — and that is where I
started writing. Now it is almost noon; I shall look for a
restaurant.   A bell rings across the street and all the
kids leave.

12:31 PM   Next improbable stop, Da La Thiem — a
Chinese restaurant on the road to Bethlehem — called
here Derek Beit Lechem — Bread House Way —
דרק בית לחם. I walked a long way through an old
Jerusalem neighborhood. I mean California-old, 50 or
100 years. Past single houses, apartment houses, schools
with high iron-bar fences, overgrown gardens.   Ah, my
corn soup.   Fortunately, I have a good city map, so I
was able to guide myself to Bethlehem Way — one of the
few streets that cross the rail track. For I am in the
neighborhood south of the rail station.   I am the only
one in this large restaurant. Can it be too early? No, it is
almost a quarter to one.   I liked walking the little
streets of this peripheral neighborhood. I felt like a
traveler, not a tourist. Can one travel through modern
neighborhoods? Somehow, it is difficult, they are full of
presenting, seem false.

12:53 PM   Three well-dressed women enter the room,
speaking — at first I thought Yiddish — but maybe it is
German. I listen carefully to catch what language the
waiter will use with them. I am not sure what I hear.
German? A few English words? The menu is in Hebrew
and English.   I finish my Mushrooms and Broccoli

and Rice. With chopsticks. My ego takes pride in using chopsticks skillfully. Two more women come in, also well dressed. This seems to be a matron's club. They are ushered in by the Chinese waitress, who wears a bright yellow blouse and black pants. She speaks a Chinese-accented Hebrew to the new arrivals. As in Madrid's Chinese restaurants — a Chinese-accented Spanish. Remarkable people — and they share traits with the Jews. Long tradition, dispersed all over the world, great respect for learning, emphasis on family, clever, hard working. But there are a billion and a quarter Chinese and only 13 million Jews.

I take off my glasses, pick at the inner corners of my eyes. That is one of the places of the body that exudes. A personal act — picking at the corners of one's eyes.

1:31 PM   I walk again. And now I sit on a bench kindly placed on the sidewalk of Beit Lechem Way for such as me. I am only about a third of the way back to Beit Shmuel. This is a pleasant-looking street — the only problem is the stream of autos going by.

1:39 PM   I have walked on a side street through a fine pleasant neighborhood of solid two-story stone houses, with big trees and pleasant gardens. The street was Yitzak Cremieux. The street I crossed before that was Lloyd George. I'd place this neighborhood in the time of the Mandate, between the wars.

1:51 PM   I sit on a bench in Liberty Bell Park — where there is reputed to be an exact replica of the American Liberty Bell. I think the motto, Proclaim Liberty Through the Land, so on, is taken from a psalm. Yes? No? The park is pleasant, large, and being embellished with more stone work, arbors, so on. Many things are labeled. Fountains from so and so and his two sons. Arbor by Mr. and Mrs. so and so. Mostly American Jews, I assume. American Jews have given greatly to the parks and institutions of Jerusalem. Here, I see a stone in the center of the arbor where-in I sit. Let's look at it. In Hebrew, and below, English, this is engraved on the stone, about one half meter square:

Garden Gift of the Helmut Kreutz Family,
Haeger-Lagenaubach, West Germany   October 1988

Here, further on, is a stone plaque set in a stone wall surrounding a courtyard with stone benches:

Provided by the Joseph R. Liss Family,
Philadelphia, Pennsylvania USA

The next little courtyard says:

In honor of Frances and Julius E. Flink, New-Jersey.
By their children and grandchildren

The next courtyard is smaller with an olive tree and wooden benches half around the tree:

The Yolanda Patio
Donated in her memory by her son Gilbert De Botton

And, at the entrance to the long arbor walk on which these courtyards are situated:

The Philip M. Klutznick Arbor

Here, at the end of the arbor, is a raised stone platform. Nearby is a stone column a meter high. On the top it says:

Bandstand contributed by the Ethel and Harry Daroff Foundation,in honor of Joseph, Michael & Samuel Daroff.

Ah, here, in line with the bandstand, is another stone platform and on it, from a six by six beam, hangs a bronze bell. Cast into the metal at the top is:

"Proclaim Liberty Throughout the Land
unto All the Inhabitants Thereof.
Lev. XXVNX."

The band underneath that says:

"By order of the

— Oh, here two young men, dressed in the black suits and black coats of the religious, come strolling by and stop to look at me as I peer up at the bell and try to make out the inscription. One says, loudly, God bless America — in sort of a matter-of-fact tone — no blessing in it. Yeah, I say — and he raises his hand to the other fellow, as if to say, What did I tell you — he's an American. (His accent was American also.) They walk on.

So — to continue —
"By order of the Assembly of the Province of Pennsylvania
for the State House in Philad A."

Underneath that it says:

"Pass and Stow
Philad A
MDCCLIII"

And there are a number of graffiti scribbled on the bell. One, in white paint, says
"JAL 2/11/15." 15? A young couple come up on the platform. They look under the bell, tap the metal. They speak Russian.

The Liberty Bell of Jerusalem

Ah, I move away from the bell. I see another stone with an inscription. I go over. It says, "Jerry the Dragon". I look up. Yes, a large fanciful stone sculpture is embedded in a great grass mound: a large stylized dragon head and a series of big humps going along the spine of the mound.

2:35 PM   I have crossed the road, which may be King David Road, and I am in the continuation of the park on the other side. I think of Alan Slifka. I admire his decision to put his money to use in improving the lot of the Arabs citizens of Israel and to promote Arab-Jewish co-existence. For this he is not having his name carved in stone in prominent places. There is nothing wrong with beautiful parks — they are very good and I honor those who make them possible. But Alan's is a more heart-filling endeavor.

2:46 PM   I walk in the park in back of the modern building next to the King David Hotel. Here are two excavations some 15 feet below the lawn surface. One is a shallow cave, with remnants of a rough stone wall at the back. The other shows a corner of a course of dressed stone blocks. I see no explanation of their significance. Now a man who looks like a guide leads a couple down into one of the excavations.

2:54 PM   I go down to the dressed stone. I see, further on, below the level of the massive stone wall, there is a stone arch and a stairway. Was this a tomb? I go down the stairs — the entrance is closed by an iron door. On it is a symbol something like this 𝛷 , if I remember right. I'd go back and look but there are three people now in the stairway. Not that this place is crowded. I am now sitting on one of the massive dressed stone blocks.

I went back and checked the symbol — it is this: 𝛷

It has become a delightful afternoon — the sunlight fills the sky and warms my back. It is quiet here — I hear one bird singing behind me, and from the Old City comes the tolling of one bell. Is it proclaiming liberty?   I shall look up that quotation. From the bronze reference, I take that it comes from Leviticus. And I have Leviticus in my massive Hebrew-English Torah, back in my room at Beit Shmuel.

[2017 note: I still have the same book in Santa Cruz. The Liberty Bell quotation is from the King James translation of the Old Testament (Leviticus, chapter

25, verse 10). This part of Leviticus sets the rules for a jubilee year, which is to happen every 50 years. My Hebrew-English Torah translates the Hebrew word as "release" rather than "liberty" and the instruction of verse 10 is to "release" all slaves in the jubilee year (apparently this rule was never actually practiced).]

As I sit here on this stone, the only other person who has been here the whole time is a woman dressed in long black skirt, black sweater and tan head covering. She sits on a stone in the lawn, about 30 meters away. I first took her to be an Arab woman. Now I am not sure. The religious Jewish women also wear head coverings like that.

It is a lovely time and place. The afternoon sun, the birds, the green grass, the long view, across the valley, of the walls of the Old City. The lowering sun is now just touching the roof of the King David Hotel and in a few minutes this spot will be in the shade. The sun does not stand still. Or is it we who do not stand still?

3:09 PM   Ah, now that I have walked on a little, I see something else. The sitting woman is wearing black slacks, not a long skirt. And I see another woman, dressed just the same. She gives a come here sign to the seated woman, who rises. What the other woman is doing is walking on the path, which is bordered by olive trees, and picking things off the ground. Olives, I assume. So, I look down as I walk the other direction on the path. All the olives I see are squashed on the stone path. Maybe this area has already been covered by the gleaners. But no. I look on the grass and here is a perfectly nice black olive. But can one eat an olive right from the tree? Don't they have to be treated? I'll take this one with me. Maybe try a tentative bite.

3:19 PM   I come out to the street near the French Consulate. Beit Shmuel is just around the bend. But it is still too nice an afternoon to go inside. Nor do I want to go past Beit Shmuel to the fractious noise and smell of the traffic on King David Road. So I turn back to this bench, near to where I sat yesterday morning, looking across to the sun-drenched wall of the Old City. Shadows of the long graceful leaves of the tree above me play across this page as I write. It is a delightful place — in spite of the constant rumble of traffic that comes from the road leading to Jaffa Gate. I think that is the road to Hebron, which was also alongside the terrace I was on yesterday. I look at my map. Yes, it is called Derek Hebron. Derek Beit Lechem (Bethlehem Way) parallels Derek Hebron (Hebron Way) and joins it at a point further along than I was today.

~ *21* ↶

Being a Mensch

And a SuperTourist: 20 centuries in 20 minutes

Jerusalem   Wednesday, November 15, 6:43 AM
Another bright day. I shall walk a bit before breakfast.

9:48 AM   Well, I must write this. This is my next-to-last day in Jerusalem. I listed things I want to do. Most of them housekeeping: go to bank to transfer money to my cousin's account, mail books home, go to the copy shop and then mail another part of this writing. Do homework for Hebrew class this afternoon. So on. And then, I thought, there are these places in the Old City I was told are very interesting. So I decided to go to the Old City. I walked down the hill, and up again on the way to Jaffa Gate. When I came to the road across from the city wall I stood with several people waiting for the light to change. One man took a picture of the city wall. And, before the light changed, I turned and started in the other direction, toward the new city, the bank, the copy shop.   I so dislike being a tourist. I'd rather just schmooze about. That is what I enjoy. Maybe it has to do with the fact that I am not, haven't been for some time, gainfully employed?

10:03 AM   The cat and the raven. The raven almost as big as the cat. I see the cat first, gray and white tiger stripes. A small cat, thin but graceful and all here. This is where it belongs, crossing the yellow paving stones. The paving stones are of the broad walkway through the old cemetery, which I have walked on many times, going to and from the city center from Beit Shmuel. I shall this time walk into the center of the cemetery. My map shows a large square pool in the middle of the cemetery.   In the middle of this walkway there is an ancient domed stone building, 20 feet high. I assume it is a tomb. Of whom? From when?

Mamilla Pool

10:11 AM   Yes, there is a very large, constructed rectangle — bigger than a football field and going down about 15 feet, stone bottom and stone sides. At one corner a stone stairway goes down. Perhaps it is an ancient reservoir? There is now a high wire fence about it. None of the graves in the cemetery has an inscription. Some are marked by several layers of old stone blocks. There are a score of cars parked through the cemetery; some may use it as cheap parking. The cemetery looks the scene of struggle between care and neglect. Scattered bottles and plastic, over spread chipped wood. Trimmed trees and weeds.

[**2017 note**: The large rectangle is called the Mamilla Pool and was part of the ancient Jerusalem water system. It was built some 2000 years ago. Around it is the ancient Mamilla Cemetery, which, says Wikipedia, contains several impressive medieval mausoleums and Sufi shrines.]

10:30 AM   Bank Hapoalim, foreign currency desk. Why do I prefer this to a preserved 70 A.D. house?

10:50 AM   On Ben Yehuda Street.   Here is a guy pushing a stroller with two four-month-old babies. And wearing a submachine gun!

11:38 AM   I did not think it would be so crowded this early. The veggie restaurant on Ben Yehuda. I now have my food; I sit up on the balcony. I feel jumpy and tense. I eat my split pea soup. At the next table a young man talks in a slow, dark, monotone. "It wears me out . . . she is so insecure" — he tells his down story in a down way. His companion has her back to me — a young woman with dark hair. She murmurs. I can't hear her words but her tone and rhythm are hopeful, helpful. Lunchtime therapy? The man's voice becomes a little more animated.

Downstairs, a few months-old baby squalls desperately, no comfort in the world. Now she quiets, I look down — her mother has picked her up, holds her close, sways gently.

Ben Yehuda St pedestrian mall

The young man at the next table leaves. The woman stays, opens a bag, takes out paper, rearranges. The man comes back. Maybe they have just arrived in the city.

I am tired, struggling inside. Something in my forearms, something in my calves. I chew too hard, I grip the pen too hard. I hold myself tightly. What is it? Too much city? Noise? Autos? Too much aloneness? The voices come up from below. A high man's voice.

The young man and young woman are still rearranging their bags. They are either coming or going. They stand. I see that he is quite tall, much taller than her. Their bags are backpacks. The girl puts on an enormous pack. Down the stairs they go, out to the street.

6:18 PM   Oh boy — I am being a mensch. The story is that I was feeling somewhat bummed out this afternoon. I studied for my Hebrew class at the Y and I didn't feel very good, physically, emotionally, spiritually — in a word bummed out. And I thought — well I really don't feel like going to the Hebrew class. I won't go, I won't pay — 140 shekels is a whole lot for three classes. I'll never see anyone, the teacher, the class, again.   Then I pulled myself up — at 4:10 PM — and gave myself a talking to — What, you went to two classes and you're not going to pay for them?

Oh, another thing I forgot to say was that, as in every beginning language class, the class had arrived at the point where students talk a little, and, always, the thing they are asked to talk about is: My Family. The teacher said, You don't have to tell the truth. So, for the class last Monday I had prepared a little talk — to give me material I invented a wife and five children, living here and there, doing this and that. But then in class everyone seemed to be bashfully telling the truth, so I didn't talk last time. And I do feel shame at not having a family. Not to go into why right now, but it's an interesting thing to think about — and — I think, a particularly Jewish thing. Not having a family puts you low in a Jewish context. Anyway — that, too, contributed to my reluctance to go to class tonight. I had rewritten my story to the true one.

But anyway — I pulled myself up and said, Now you march right out of here to that class and you pay whatever they ask and you participate — and no back talk! So. I went to the Y, went to the desk to pay — No, she said, you must give us a note from the teacher saying how much before we can take payment. So I went to class. And liked it a lot. This teacher, Rachel, is very good. And I told my story, in Hebrew. Then, at the end of the class, I told her — I need a note from you as to how much I should pay. She wrote a note in Hebrew. I looked at it, the figure was 190.   I thought maybe she didn't remember that I wasn't staying for the whole course, and she had said 140 on Monday. So I said, Maybe I should pay only for a month because this is my last class.   Your last class? she said.   Yes, I said, I leave Jerusalem on Friday.   Oh, she said, well then forget it.   Ah, I said, I should pay something.   No, no, she said, forget it.   Thank you, I said.   Have a good trip and continue learning, she said.   So — I was a mensch and she was a mensch. A mensch mensch this and a mensch mensch that. And we live happily ever after. And I feel good.

Jerusalem   Thursday, November 16, 11:14 AM
I have been a long time at the main post office. Sending books. Some 8.5 kilos of books, if I read the receipt correctly. This will be a great weight off mind and body on the way home. I also sent back to David, my erstwhile teacher, the book on History of the Jews, and the kippa he had loaned me. I am paying my debts to society. Here is a little guy with a toy airplane in the line in front of me. Waiting in line is very hard for little kids.

12:20 PM   Japanese restaurant. In the old section, not far from Café Tmol Shilshom.

2:25 PM   Just a note. I am wandering through the cemetery again. This time on the other side of the large empty pool.

4:33 PM   I am doing a last day run about the Old City. I am now drinking that old favorite — mango juice — nervously as I wait for the Russian movie to finish. Then I can go in and look at the 70 A.D. house. I finally found it. But it closes at five. So I have 20 minutes to do 20 centuries. No problem. I drink mango juice and Ka Pow — SUPER TOURIST appears. Able to leap 20 centuries in the blink of an eye.   A stream of Russians comes forth — right on schedule.   Here goes.

∽ *22* ∾
Ten Hours to Madrid

Doesn't seem a very sane way of life

Ben Gurion Airport   Friday, November 17, 5:40 AM
Airport morning. Leaving Jerusalem two hours ago,
yellow lights in the night. The van came at 3:45 AM — I
had expected it at 4 AM. The hotel fellow knocked at my
door, and I zipped my suitcase and hurried down. It was
exciting being in the van in the night, picking up more
passengers on a residential street corner, then heading
out of the city on streets I knew and streets I didn't know.
There is my boarding call.

5:56 AM   On the bus going out to the plane. Light
coming over the sky.

6:02 AM   On the plane, seat 26-8 — my, what big
engines you have, grandma airplane. Oh, it is warm —
off with the wool sweater. I stand up, pull my sweater up
and off. I never learned to take a sweater off gracefully
— crossed arms and so on. I just tug til it comes over my
head.   I yawn. I was in bed at 8 PM last night but slept
waiting for 3 AM.

My time at Beit Shmuel was good. I slept peacefully — to bed about 9 PM every night and slept warm, quiet and secure, and woke around 6 PM. I constructed little rituals of the day: Up for a morning walk in the city — before the autos take over from morning, buy *The Jerusalem Post* and the *International Herald Tribune*. Come back to Beit Shmuel for the buffet breakfast — take a plate — big helping of tomatoes and cucumbers and cottage cheese, a tiny bowl of cornflakes and milk, three slices of bread and a cup of tea.

The plane is moving — seven minutes before the scheduled departure time. The lights go out. My seatmate points out rain clouds coming in from the sea.

6:25 AM   Up in the air, into the clouds, toward the light. Four and something hours to Paris. The plane levels and circles over Tel Aviv. Now I see color in the sky — morning blue and gold. The little girl in front of me — two years old? — turns on her light. And off. And on. Now the plane wing, inside of which I sit, is gold and the sky is gray. I turn on my light — the light is bright, harsh. The plane bounces a bit. I shall read *The Jerusalem Post*.

9:44 AM   I trust Paris is down there.   All Europe is covered by cloud today. We are going into la soupe.

10:51 AM   Somewhere in an airport, somewhere in France. Eating a thick slice of rye bread. Imported. From Jerusalem by me. Cabeza — that's it. I have a headache. Dolor de ???. I couldn't think of the Spanish word for head. Tete. Rosh in Hebrew. But the Spanish didn't come — until just now. The schedule says "snack" on the Iberia flight to Madrid — from 11:45 AM to 1:45 PM. I guess in Spain 1:45 PM is too early for lunch.

But I have my rye bread. Plus one apple and one persimmon. And a Swiss Army knife. I am hungry. The lounge I sit in is identical to the one I sat in at the break on my flight Boston-Paris-Tel Aviv. There are no ranks of seats as in most US airports, but a curving bench of stuffed seats all around the perimeter of this large room, plus a similar long bench curving through the center of the room. The floor is made of those tiny hexagonal tiles that I think of as a floor of a turn-of-the-century middle-class French restaurant.

Flying violates norms of time and space. I am in Jerusalem in the middle of the night, I sit in a long box for four hours and now I am in a very different place, with a headache, eating rye bread from Jerusalem. Doesn't seem a very sane way of life. I could bike to Capitola for four hours and eat rye bread on the beach.

People from a flight — from Amsterdam, I think — walk into the room through a doorway in back of me. A little blond boy wants to play with the air conditioning vents. He explains to his mother, in Dutch, I think. She holds out her hand, waiting calmly. He runs and catches up to her.

So — it is now 11:23 AM and no sign yet of the Iberia airplane. Iberia pilots have been on intermittent strike all this month. They didn't work Tuesday and Wednesday of this week, but they are supposed to work today.

11:53 AM   On the plane, seat 10F. Joy — I have a window seat and the aisle seat is vacant. And I just got a copy of today's *El Pais*. I feel myself entering familiar

Spain as I look at the front page of *El Pais*.

12:08 PM   We leave French soil, and soil French air. Ooh, what a pretty country. Sun and shadow, kelly green and white, city and country. We float with the big white clouds. Oh my, why not stick with French in France, live the fat life?

I look down on the white clouds — nothing becomes something or something becomes something else. This is no ordinary thing — looking down on clouds. Terrible thing to treat it as ordinary. But I have a headache, me duele la cabeza.

∼ *23* ∽
Madrid and the Farm

A wistfulness, a muted anguish, in these yellow leaves

Still Friday, 1:35 PM   About to land in Madrid. France is green; España is brown. But not just brown — red brown, olive brown, shadow brown, yellow brown, gray brown, tree brown, dry brown, mud brown, road brown — a symphony in brown.   Today España has lines and rows of clouds marching regularly across it. We come down to cloud line. White.   Now under — dark and white.   Rolling rolling.   Trees like a thousand nipples on the rolling land. Sensuous curves. Rough curves. The wheels are down.   Busy road, white houses. A stream — lots of chocolate water.   So — after a few hours in green, I have returned to dry land.

2:15 PM   On the airport bus.   New redbrick apartment buildings. I am very tired.   A building with blue mirrored windows and a fountain. "Pretentious" says the *Times*, "Ugly" says the *Herald*.   I don't think this is such a great idea — the way I scheduled my return flights. In five days will I have recovered and be ready to fly again? And then four days after that, again? No se, nadie sabe. Ani lo yodea.

2:51 PM   In a cab — approaching Avenida de la Albufera. This familiar city, familiar trees and buildings. Back to Boyle Heights, East Los Angeles. The root and origin. I think I either ought to travel a good deal more or a good deal less. More — in that coming from Jerusalem, I see Madrid differently. I layer, compare, infuse — it becomes richer. Less — all the world is in Concord — or in Santa Cruz. All the richness. Right? Wrong?   Now we pass the football stadium of the Vallecas Rayos. Is that the name?   Soon we will pass Alcampo, the superstore.

[**A 2017 background note on Spain:** I met Pepin in 1983. From October 1986 to February 1987 I lived in Madrid and helped Pepin, Celso and Emilio buy the old dairy farm between Huete and Carrascosa del Campo in the La Mancha region (about 70 miles east of Madrid) which they turned into El Colmenar (The Apiary), the farm-school for maginados (people on the margin of society, mostly ex-drug addicts) of their Escuelas para la Vida. Before 1995, I visited Spain again in '84, '86–'87, '88, '90, '91, '92 and '94. Pepin, Celso and Emilio visited me in Santa Cruz in August 1991 and again in March 1995.]

Approaching Carrascosa del Campo   Saturday, November 18, 10:56 AM
The sky ahead is dark gray. The land breathes moisture. Wet, ready to live. Or is that a California sentiment? For here, the cold doesn't allow winter green. But today one can believe Californian. For there will be rain, there has been rain. And it is not cold.   The old tunnel, the river bluffs across. Very old rocks. Monuments to time. The dark clouds ragged over the hills on the horizon — it is

raining there now. The land is a rich orange-red brown, with pastel yellow browns, dry greens. This is familiar, comfortable. A truck ahead, we slow a little, then swing out into the opposite lane and pass. I feel the dangerous sweetness in my mouth from the "borracho"— the sweet flat roll we bought at the old bakery in Tarancon. It has been there for 200 years, said Pepin. Passed on in the family, one to the other. And this roll — they make others, he said, but this is typical of Tarancon. As I look down and write, the white line flashes up from the roadway. Carrascosa. We no longer go through the town to find the road to Huete.

Ralph, Pepin, Emilio, Celso in Tarancon

1:43 PM Sitting on a familiar armchair in the community room at the granja (farm). I have walked about with Celso for an hour. The flowers, the new terrace, the grapevines, the invernaderos (greenhouses). Besides me in this room there are three others. One

Above: Walking on the road near the Farm - Emilio in blue, Pepin in red.

Below: Celso, Pepin, Manuel, Ralph, and Emilio

playing *Silent Night* on the flute. This is practice for Christmas. Most of the rest of the guys are in the building below practicing the Christmas obra de teatro, which is a full length play with six characters called *Escuadron de la Muerte* (*Squadron of Death*).   And — I am hungry.

3:59 PM   Back in the community room. After dinner and after walking up the hill to watch the football game of the fellows here. It rains lightly outside, the sky is a lighted gray, the wind is shown by the agitation of the yellow leaves I see through the window. In here, it is shadow and brown tone — not gloomy but blocked out in shadow and stretches of light. Light given in a different way from sun light — everything is solid in itself, not drawn out or washed away by sun light.

5:51 PM   About to watch a movie, *Nell*, in the lower building.

8:22 PM   Back again in the community room. The TV on.   Almost everyone of the community here, sitting about the perimeter of the room on the couches and armchairs. Strangely hungry again. And feeling concern and connection.

9:36 PM   Well — so to bed — not much time for writing today.

El Colmenar (the farm)   Sunday, November 19, 10:49 AM
Sitting on a rough log bench on the terrace in front of the main house. Behind me I hear the bell of the cow. I turn around. Yes, across the little valley, on the path that goes along the fence near the pigpen. Black and white, her

head down at the base of the fence. In front of me, one of the dogs lies on the terrace. For, now — between the cold morning and the rain – there is sunshine. A winter sun, very welcome — by dog and cow and me. Emilio walks by quickly, intent, frowning a little. And here comes another dog.

1:14 PM   When I have time to write here — like now, waiting for lunch — the uppermost in my mind is "I am hungry". I sit again on one of the rough log benches. I pause. Much to write but the hunger is in my stomach, in my hand, in my head. I woke before seven, and then had a cup of warm milk and a couple hunks of bread. I walked a mile or two, sat in on the practice of the play — which was hard — listening, trying to capture meaning from the quick-spoke Spanish.

3:21 PM   Down the sunshine road — stony fields plowed, pale hills rolling away. A silent, pastel land. I have passed this way many times, many days. We reach the main road and turn right, toward Huete. The sun follows us, the silent hills roll alongside. Now!! the hills exclaim, green bushes rise up, colored leaves say time is passing. Even the State, whatever State now exists and thinks itself forever, has marked time passing, by rebuilding the road. We reach the beginning of Huete, the park of yellowing leaves, still remembering the green of summer.   There is a wistfulness, a muted anguish, in these yellow leaves. For lives yellow like leaves, and there will be new leaves.   We are now on the rough road to the old molino (mill).

4 PM   Gone — the old mill. Now but a pile of stones, a stock of old timber, the weathered pink tiles laid one atop the other.   Back we go on the bumpy road.

Celso with the tiles from the old molino

Okay — now we are on the high way, the broad way, the smooth way. Past the park of aged leaves, on the way to Carrascosa del Campo. No one smokes now in the little van, but my throat burns with cigarettes past. In my stomach, the spaghetti and tomato paste, oil and onions sit uneasily, not welcomed. It is a day of darkness and light. The round brown hills dark against the gray and white sky. We speed along the black pavement. The land says something but I can't hear it clearly, my ears are listening to spaghetti.

Now on to Madrid. This is a day of endings. The sun is barred by the gray sky. The end of the sun. The fields and hills are barred by some indistinct face of time.   Two women walk along the side of the road. Just here, we take the bypass road that goes around Carrascosa. The old church is there, but we don't see it, we don't pass the bakery and the two cafés, the bare little plaza. The fields are a yearning red-brown and tan-brown, neatly plowed, waiting for a new time, another time.

I came to Spain, twelve years back, near the beginning of the building and the bustling — the new roads, expressways, high-rises. I saw a lot of it. I won't see it finished.

Ah, here is the old tunnel, the river, the railroad — all at the same place of the road.   I cough a little.   Tile roofs, yellow-gold leaves. A grove of evergreens trimmed like French poodles — all the lower branches cut away. A faintly terraced hill. Who made the terraces — to what end? The auto and the road, neither apart nor together do they know. Now I see on the horizon a tall grain elevator — it is Tarancon, where we will join the Valencia-Madrid expressway. We cross the railway one last time. Madrid 84, says one sign. Centro Urbano, another — with an arrow. Restaurante El Cruce. Fiat. Opel. Mercedes-Benz. Restaurante Los Manchegos, Bodas. Mueblas de Caña. Picina Municipal. And now the wistful land again. An olive grove.

We are on the expressway. I remember the two-lane road. No one remembers a Roman pike. Memory doesn't age well. But is there a racial memory? There is a blocked-out brownstone church on a nearby hill — does it have racial memory? Those Jews in the black, brimmed hats in Jerusalem claim to remember the tablet stones at Sinai. It comes along, one to the other, the direct line of transmission. That's what David told me — the problem with Jesus, he said, is that he began to talk while his teacher still spoke — didn't wait for the transmission. There is a tan dirt road rounding the hill, leading away to the right — the north?

Suddenly, I feel tired. I have run out of spaghetti energy. Or maybe all my energy has been used up digesting spaghetti. I look around. Everyone in the car but me and the driver is asleep. Pepin, lying in back, in the baggage area. Manuel and Celso, with me in the back seat. And Emilio in front. They have been on this road hundreds of times. They feel they know the little green bushes, the dry sweep to the higher hills, the power lines, the gray road, the moving horizon.   I cough. My head swims a little.

We are not meant to move this fast, with the white line flashing beneath us. Another olive grove — lonely trees by a lonely road. Not that there are few autos on the road — there are many. But there are few people. People in autos aren't people — at least to those not in the auto with them.

A town, with many new white-walled, red-roofed buildings approaching the road. The new Spain: a dry France, a European America. And we rush along. The land swells and eases, swells and eases, the road cuts straight and gray. I feel the van ready to spin and roll, and it doesn't. The driver presses, all the other drivers press. I push up my glasses, try to make out the speed. We come to a long hill and slow, pass a long blue truck. The hill eases, we gather speed. As fast as we can, that's how fast we go. What reason is there not to? Life goes from A to B, speed is one answer. Who knows other answers? The olive trees flash by, the muscles in my forehead tingle, my legs tighten. Three cars pass us, and are quickly gone from sight.

Everyone sleeps on. The sky is a little grayer, the road

less gray. Ah, here is the place where a vast lower land appears. Always I am here reminded of the long view of the Sacramento Valley when coming down from the Sierras, at above Folsom.

A little white tin box speeds by our little white tin box. Madness is the rage. We are coming to cross el rio Tajo. I see the high bluff along the far side of the river. A blue building next to a red building.   I look ahead, see a car merging into our lane. We don't slow. No problem. Ah, here are little tan boxes of houses, rank on rank they march to the highway. Oh, I don't like this speedy ride. The low gray hills alongside cry with me. They are being filled with rubble.

Now I see a block of red brick towers, we are not far from Madrid. The traffic has thickened up, setting like pudding.   It is 5:08 PM — but, unlike Israel, it is not dark here at five. Ah, now I see stacks of red brick ahead — we are almost at the pueblo of Vallecas, where we will leave the expressway to take Celso home. I see the tall chimney of a power plant in the distance.   No, we didn't go off to the pueblo of Vallecas — we have come around further to the neighborhood of (same name) Vallecas. 5:16 We arrive.

~ *24* ⌒

Here and There in Madrid

Familiar spaces and favorite places

Madrid   Monday, November 20, 6:23 AM
Different country, different light. In Madrid at this hour
it is black night and the world sleeps. In Jerusalem it
is bright day and beginning bustle. I went to sleep last
night at 8:30 and was awake at 5:45. I look at the pile
of clothes to be washed; I have a disorder on the floor. I
opened my two little bags and everything inside doubled
in volume and popped out, spread forth, and there is
the disorder. But atop the clothes to wash, what is it I
see and don't recognize in the dim light of the small
fluorescent lamp? It is blue-green and points up. Oh.
Yes. It is, of course, a large blue-green and white stuffed
rabbit and it is two ears that point up. Stuffed animals
— muñecas. Everyone gives them to Emilio, Celso and
Pepin — so there are several atop the beds at the farm.
And Emilio has them on his bed here. I am in Emilio's
room. He is at the farm.

10:04 AM   On the Metro. Leaving station Miguel
Hernandez. And it is warm — the subway car is
overheated. I hope, that with developing wealth, the

Spanish will not begin to heat interior spaces. That would make wearing long underwear untenable.

I don't feel it here in the Metro car. But when I walked the street from Pepin's piso (apartment) to the Metro station, I felt it: The sense of being in a familiar space. And more than that. The sense of having lived here. Through time. Across time. I was here when there were no towering redbrick buildings on the far side of Avenida de la Albufera. I was here when the newspaper kiosk was in a different place. I have been here in hot times and cool. I have been here in the rain. I have changed, I have seen changes. And I have seen the continuity. The same neatly dressed, carefully groomed, stout woman who now passes along in the car — I have seen her before. Maybe not her. Maybe not this bird, that yellow leaf. But I have seen the birds and the leaves. Is that true? Have I? Or is it just a lazy perception — that sees the same bird, the same leaf — and even lazier not to see a new and different person?

The train clicks along, the stations come and go. We may be approaching — yes — Atocha Renfe — the main rail station — now connected right into the Metro stop. I shall go to Puerta del Sol — center city. For I want to walk to Plaza Santa Ana to check on small hotels that we might stay in next May. I shall be a guide, the complete tour guide. It is an interesting role. Something more than wandering about. Something with purpose, applying my wandering experience, planning, reading. I like that sort of thing — constructing a whole, having the outline. Yet, of course, allowing for the spontaneous, the unexpected.

[2017 note: Here is what the tour guide reference is about: The farm near Huete was bought by Escuelas

para la Vida in 1987. The only building then on it, a large
concrete-block dairy barn was rebuilt into a residence
with some dozen bedrooms, bathroom, kitchen, dining
room, classroom and community room. In the early 90s
another large residence building was built on the other
side of the farm's narrow valley. That building was
used mainly for volunteers and parents and family who
came on weekends. Pepin and I talked of also using this
building to provide revenue for the farm. I had the idea of
bringing groups interested in the work and in seeing this
part of Spain. I thought (mistakenly) Elder Hostel might
be interested. I proposed to bring a group to the farm in
the spring of 1996 to test the idea. I was not successful;
in the end the only person I brought was my friend Rita
(who was one recipient of the original Long Letters).

I think the area of the farm very pretty in late May
when there is the green of the winter wheat and the red
poppies blooming, and also in the Fall. And the history of
the area is fascinating. Huete was important in Roman
times as a center for mining mica — which Romans used
for window panes and, when crushed, to cover arena
floors. There are Roman ruins not far away at Segobriga.
In Reconquest times (750 to 1492), Huete was often a
Christian stronghold opposed to Moslem Cuenca. The
headquarters of the Order of Santiago, one of the large
religious-military orders of the Reconquest, still stands
nearby at Ucles (the father of the fifteenth century poet
Jorge Manrique was a grand master of the order). And
Cervantes has Don Quixote passing close to Huete as
he traveled through La Mancha on his chivalric route to
Barcelona.]

The train stops. I twist my neck to see where. Tirso de
Molino. I don't have to worry. I will know Sol without

looking. For there'll be a great movement out of people in the car. The woman in the brown slacks standing in front of me will go out the door.

10:20 AM   No, she didn't. I sit on a bench on the platform. Beside me a sullen young fellow with a backpack on the seat at his side.

12:34 PM   An old favorite — and the best seat in the house. It's the Cerveceria Alemana. And I sit at the window table, looking out at the peaches and cream façade of the theater — could I call it the National Theater? Maybe — I have never gone there. But that is where, I think, are staged the works of Lope de Vega and Tirso de Molino and — who are the others of la Edad de Oro?

I shall look at El Pais, which I carry in my ever-present shoulder bag.

1:15 PM   Still at Cerveceria Alemana. I must get myself together, pay, leave Cerveceria Alemana, walk to Sol, take the Metro to Vallecas. For lunch will be served at 2 PM.

1:33 PM   Metro, line 1, once again. Back, back, against the grain of time. And the white cord hangs from my fly. But one doesn't want to fumble with one's fly on the Metro. I don't know what the white cords are for. These pants are beltless, with elastic. And that works fine. But — in addition — there is the white cord that goes through the slot in the waistband, all the way around, with plastic tips like shoelaces. Both ends just hang there and pop out above the waistband — and I stuff them back in. But the worst is when one of them gets zipped into my fly and then hangs out the top of the fly. That is what I think has happened — after I went to the bathroom at Cerveceria Alemana. I first went to the bathroom, and then sat at one of the marble table. With my dignity gathered round me like a Roman toga — for that is the way one is at Cerveceria Alemana. The place demands it. And I did not know that a white string five inches long was hanging out from my fly. Sic Transit Dignity.

Ah — we arrive at the next to last stop and only one other person sits in the car — at the other end. Now — I pull up my sweater and look. No — it is not coming out from my fly, it is coming over the waistband. Much better. And this is not the next to last stop — second from last. Now I am the only one in this Metro car. Total privacy. A rare thing in the city. Like being the only one on an elevator.

2:17 PM Waiting. For dinner. For dinner to arrive, it is necessary that the other diners arrive. That is, Pepin and Manuel. The other two diners are here, present and accounted for. Me. And Celso, the cook, who sits in the other rocking chair — at a right angle to mine. And the sounds come up, distantly, from below. Children piping and yelling, slam of a gate, a truck going by. But mostly the children — the future's noise. And there is sunlight on the red-brick walls. The day started with less sunlight. But the trend is right — toward light.

I am not growling — stomach growling — hungry. That is due to the two bananas and the small bread — bosillo — that I ate before I went to Cerveceria Alemana.

It is such a pleasure to walk into a little store and say ¿Hay platanos? (Are there bananas?) or Quisiera un pan pequenito (I would like a very small bread), instead of mumble, point and gesticulate. Of course, it takes enormous effort to be able to do that. And then you travel a few hundred miles and you are back to mumble and point. There is need for a manner of universal communication. The Chinese were reaching for it with the picture drawings.

Hmmm — lightbulb. Why not develop a little hand computer which presents all sorts of simple pictures? Can that be done? Where is a bank?: picture of a bank. Is there a universally recognized type of bank building? And then some kind of direction indicator. And then a question mark. Or — start with the question mark? I think it can be done. Look at all the highway signs. All those sentences that are in a travel phrase book — can they be put into a universally understood picture language?

[2017 note: A good 1995 idea, but now the mobile phone apps have leapfrogged past it.]

I yawn. Why I don't know — since I have slept nine hours each of the past three nights. My goodness, my visit to Spain is more than half over. The time does pass.

7:15 PM   The lights go by and the lights stand still. Lights and lights. Blue-white and yellow bright, red and green. Pink. The big red light up high says Hotel Mediodia. Great clusters of yellow lights on very high standards give me light to write by. We stand on the sidewalk beyond Atocha station. Cars go this way and that, although most go unseen in the tunnel underneath us. In front of us is spread the word of the world: Prensa y Revistas — a newspaper kiosk. On the other side of the walk a woman roasts chestnuts over a round brazier. I buy some in a paper cone and share them with Celso, Manuel and Pepin, who stand with me here.

Why are we standing here? I don't know. I have nothing better to do and I'm perfectly happy to stand. Probably we are waiting for the bus that Celso will take.   I asked. No, we are waiting to meet someone who will be here between 7 and 7:30. So. And it is not cold. That is why we can stand here and all Madrid can walk in the night, on the sidewalks along the streets full of autos.

Here people are walking fast. A bus, a train — something to meet, to be on time for. Two old ladies, dressed in comfortable, sensible suits, walk by, arm in arm. A young man carries a violin case, another walks by talking into a cellular phone. Every once in a while I think of my nearly new, merely blue, sweater and lift my rear from the dirty — is it dirty? — wall I lean against. Two kids on skateboards. I tire of the weight of my shoulder bag. Slip it off my shoulder, hold it between my legs. A fast-walking man in a dark suit, carrying a black notebook. Two more ladies, arm in arm. A kid in faded blue jeans. A young man, white sweater, blue shorts, running. A siren in the distance. A man in a tan raincoat. Two kids on roller skates. And the autos go by.

The short woman with white hair is taking magazines off the racks along the newspaper kiosk, handing them to someone inside. A man goes by, walking young, fast and jaunty — somewhere to go, something to show. Lots of taxis go by — all of them painted the same: white with one diagonal red stripe. Closing up the newspaper kiosk goes slowly. One box, another box, a few magazines, several newspapers. Are they closing, or only rearranging? Flashing yellow lights, pulsing wail — an ambulance goes by.

7:57 PM   On the Metro. People, in and out. People go by. People gone by. Agnes, I think: I shall ask if Agnes is seen. But Agnes is long ago. Maybe ten years ago. More people have passed me by here, in all my intermittence, than have passed me by in California, in my permanence. The velocity is much greater here, and the intensity, life and death, coming and going. Two small boys sit across from me — both wearing juvenile sweatsuits — one green and pink, the other tan and blue — and now they leave. I look about for the station name. Alto de Avenal — the next to last station.

Madrid   Tuesday, November 21, 9:56 AM
I sit on a bench on Avenida de la Albufera. In front is La Union Bar-Café. Next to it is a branch of the savings bank Caja de Madrid. Beside me on the bench are Manuel and Celso. They talk, I write. Pepin is in the Caja de Madrid. The sun shines like a giant spotlight at the top of the Avenue. People walking down the sidewalk cast long shadows before them. The world goes down here. Down to the Puente — where once there was a bridge.

10:22 AM   On the Metro. About to leave, at Puerta del Sol. Pepin and the others left at Atocha. They are to meet with a young woman from Burgos who wants to work at Pan Bendito.

[2017 note: Pan Bendito is a Gypsy neighborhood in Madrid where Pepin, Celso and Emilio set up a school for kids in a space the government rented to them. Guys from the farm and other volunteers ran it. It had to fold after a couple years — too difficult. An interesting story.]

10:27 AM   Now on the platform of Line 2. Just before I left the Line 1 car, a young man came on with an accordion. I am a father, unemployed, he said, and went down the length of the car.

~ *25* ᔆ

Madrid — Retiro Park

I live curled up in my liver, soft in Autumn russet

Still Tuesday, 11:40 AM   On a bench in Retiro Park. By the fountain at the corner of the Tanque (which means tank, cistern) — the big square pond. An October day of late November. The trees are not ablaze — that would be too strong a word. The color is gold and bronze and green-yellow. A muted color, a parting color, a rather sad color. Change and passing on. An old lady and an old dog walk by, slowly, tenderly, gingerly. It is a little cool — but I sit in the shade, as I am warm from walking in the city. A stout, buffalo-shouldered man walks by. Bald, grey fringe, pudgy face. He looks very Jewish to me. Yet very Spanish and, I am sure, as Catholic as the Pope. The old men walk slowly with their hands clasped behind their backs.

I feel tired, slightly hungry. I dwell somewhere down and inside. Maybe in my liver. I live curled up in my liver, soft soft in autumn russet, and I hear the blood gurgle pleasantly about me. I am of no mind to disturb myself, to talk or run. For now, this is fine. Maybe — I look up — maybe the gurgle of blood is the splash of the fountain in front of me? I don't want to think about that — it is much too complicated. It would tug me out from my liver, maybe up to my heart, with all the hurry and worry that goes on there.

Retiro Park in autumn

Here is a pigeon waddling past me. There — that seems an appropriate speed.   Oh my — here are two blue-suited police, wearing blue baseball-type caps. On horses. And with cellular phones — or police radio? Radio equipped horses. Everything is up-to-date in Madrid city.

12:02 PM   I watch for my compañeros — we are to meet here at noon. I hope I am in the right place. Here are two more men on horses. These two men wear what looks like regular police uniforms: dark blue jacket, light blue shirts, visored hats.

A boy stumble-walks behind me. Another boy walks alongside him. A man walks in front of me, he glances at the stumbling boy, glances away. The look on his face — what is it? Contempt? Disgust? — well, yes, faintly. It is separation. It says: The boy is not normal. I am. I have enough doubt about myself, enough trouble managing my own life — heading to oblivion — I have enough without identifying with someone who is not normal.

That is what I admire so much about Pepin and Celso. They don't glance away. There is now a fellow at the farm who is an alcoholic — 62 years old. His wife doesn't want to have anything to do with him, nor does his brother. They (Pepin and Celso) take him in.

Here goes a crowd of three-year-olds. And now, two police on motorcycles.

12:14 PM   I turn, look about. Could I be at the wrong place? I am near the corner of el Tanque, the fountain, at the end of the walk from the entrance Alcala. I think they are just a bit late. They want to talk here in the park with the young woman from Burgos. Pepin has his summer office here — on a bench of the park. In winter he goes to the enclosed, palm-tree-planted and heated old Atocha station

4:58 PM   Sitting on a little couch. In Celso's house. Having eaten well, walked about. Waiting for Pepin's call. He is at the dentist. He is to call and then we will meet him at Al Campo. Al Campo is the big grocery/clothing/etc. store in Vallecas. So, we sit here, talking Castillano, the clock ticking — outside, the children run, an auto motor. The light of day is going — to wherever lights go. Gloomy doomy dusk gathers in the corners, creeps along the walls. And the moving pen writes.

My stomach feels content after a nice lunch of a thick puree — too thick to call soup — of potatoes, squash and carrots — with some oil, some garlic? — I must try to make it at home. And chicken, salad, fruit and poleo — which I think is peppermint tea. Isabel gathered the poleo herself on the banks of the river at Avila.

Celso is now going through old papers. Something of 1980. And he tears it up. Something 15 years old has 15 years of sacred time. Can one easily tear it up? Not me. Things he wrote — poems, rip-ramp — paper gone, poem gone. Ai — I should do that. Tear up yesterday. Go on to tomorrow. Yesterday. Today. And tomorrow. Which is which? Which is real? Do yesterday and tomorrow erase today? A Christmas card of 1987. He has not yet torn it up. No. He puts it back in the old tan briefcase.

6 PM In the bus. Here is a billboard. Todos somos — I'll say it in English: We are all equal before AIDS. Now we are on Avenida de la Albufera, before the great red-brick buildings. SNAP — opens the bus door. More authority than SNAP — call it CRACK/THUMP. Peach clouds blossom from the blue evening sky. A little boy and his grandmother leave the bus. He stands quietly as she ties down the hood that goes over his head. Little kids wear puffed-up jackets with puffed-up hoods. Although it is still relatively balmy. I have the window next to me open four inches and I welcome the freshness.

Madrid Airport   **Wednesday, November 22,**
10:57 AM
The day before Thanksgiving — busiest air travel day

of the year. Is it? And here sits the air traveler. Hot. And bothered about glasses. I don't know which glasses I have on my head. Long-distance? Reading? Spare reading? I examine, compare. Yes, I have been wearing my scratched-lens old reading glasses, through which everything appears as in a fog. How did I wear these scratched lenses all the years? What else do I do that is inexplicable to a reasonable person?   There is the call for my flight, TWA 903 to New York.

11:12 AM   Aboard. Seat 21-1. Doesn't look — yet — like the busiest day in here. So. Here I am, in Spain, and out of Spain. Pepin, Celso and Manuel came with me to the airport. We took a cab on Avenida de la Albufera, right down M-40 expressway to the airport. Less time, less bother, same cost as a cab to Plaza Colon where the bus leaves for the airport. In fact it took only 15 minutes.

I said no need to accompany me to the airport. But when the cab came, Pepin was clear — we all go to the airport. They waited while I checked in. We walked up and down talking of plans — the trip in May, the possibility that the expert on AIDS they met in San Francisco in March would give a conference at the farm, whether the intelligence-boosting professor I met in Jerusalem would visit the farm.

I wanted to keep the talk going because Pepin becomes very sad at leavings. Feelings come up with Pepin. But they also swirl about in his body — mostly stress, nervousness, anxiety.

Last night I called José Manuel and Lola in Bilbao. After I talked a while with José Manuel, Pepin talked with him. After, we sat at the table. José Manuel, Pepin said, doesn't do much anymore. (José Manuel is as much a saint as Pepin. Whenever I meet him and Lola there are a couple ex-prisoners with them, for lunch or tea or to walk about town. And they took in the two teenage girls whose mother had killed herself, raised them as their own.) Es quemado, said Pepin — he is burned — that's what we say here — quemado.

I thought of Pepin. Is there some way, I asked him last night, that you can have a year of rest — perhaps arrange things at the farm so there are fewer people or more stable people? It is very hard, he said. There is no one — Antonio is very unreliable. (Antonio is the young priest of Huete, who was one of the people who took over while Pepin, Celso and Emilio were in California in March of this year.) The Ministry asked us for documents, receipts, from 1991, said Pepin, and Antonio was to deliver them and he lost them. He said they were stolen from his car, but here in Spain who robs papers? He simply lost them and makes up a story — like a child.

Now, he said, I don't know what we will do with the Ministry. There is this clause in the agreement when we bought the additional parcel of land that it would not be used for 30 years for any other purpose. You bought another parcel? I asked. Yes, up above, in the valley leading to the road. And, with Otermin, who had been in prison and a paper had to be presented, Antonio had it and every day Otermin's mother called him about it — a month passed before we got the paper. Antonio is very irresponsible.

Well — hope springs — it is a couple minutes before this airplane departs and the seat next to me is still empty.

I'll tell you the kind of problems that come up, said Pepin. That I worry about all night and can't sleep. Meecha, she is a good person, but she has a problem. (Meecha was with Pepin in the University program for a masters degree in treatment of drug addiction. I met her for the first time Saturday when she unexpectedly "dropped in" at the farm, with an Argentinian man and one other person and several bags of supplies for the farm — rice, canned goods, etc.)

Oh — no such luck — my seatmate arrives at the ultimate minute. Oh no — she goes to sit across the aisle. I think because her bag wouldn't fit under the seat. Eight hours and five minutes, the temperature in New York is 38 degrees, says the Voice. So — we are almost on our way. Long, long way.

Meecha, said Pepin, she is a good person, but this man, the Argentinian, who came to the farm with Meecha — the man is a ladron (robber), international, on a high level. I cannot have someone like that coming to the farm. What if he becomes friends with one of the boys, who then leaves with him and becomes involved in this kind of high-level robbery? This is a problem that comes from nowhere. And I can't sleep. I must call Meecha and tell her that this person cannot come to the farm.

I didn't like the Argentinian, I said, because when the chavales (boys) were giving a preview of their villancicos (Christmas songs) he talked all the time they were singing. Este me da rabia, said Pepin, that enrages me — when they show disrespect for the boys. But what can I do? I can't cause a commotion; I have to maintain equilibrium. When I cannot sleep all night and I wake with a headache, I cannot go out and say I feel terrible;

I must maintain a smile and good temper and be of help. It is very hard. I'll give you another example. You know Chon is in terrible trouble. She is ruined.

Ah, we are in the take-off lane.

∾ *26* ∾

To the Ozarks

Sitting on a jet engine, moving with thunder and fire.

Still Wednesday 12:05 PM   Here is the roar and the run — faster — and up — into the sky. Dark rain clouds and bright blue patches ahead. We go to meet them. Wow — what presumption. That is why flying scares people. It is so presumptuous. To dare to consort with dark rain clouds and the sky above.

We come to the cloud's level. Shake and shudder. Wing to cloud. We level, fly under. Oh my. Dark and light. Land and sky. Drifting mist. Dense gray. Wing down, turning. Now the sun in my eyes. Clouds below, clouds above. The purest blue — God's own blue. White mist again. We shudder through. Now a whole field, an entire world, of cloud below us. Ice-blue sky and one enormous flat grey cloud above us. We fly clear of it. Glimpses of shadowed brown land below. I am over the wing — I always seem to be over the wing. Well, better with wings than without, no?

12:12 PM   We are finally launched. We are sky creatures, thin-air creatures, sun blue creatures.

Launched over the many-humped and curled backs of cloud gods.

So, where was I? Chon. Chon has been a good friend to the farm over the last eight years. She ran the shop in Huete that sold tickets in the national lotteries. What happened to her I didn't get clearly. But it seems there were two things. One, a large sum of money in the lottery account in the bank was taken out illegally, maybe on a forged signature. Second, she sold a ticket that was a winner, and he was to pay later, but he didn't. The lottery shop is now closed. Chon apparently owes a lot of money and there seems to be some legal proceeding against her.

There was, Pepin said, this juicio (judgment?) — against Chon. We loaned some money to her — just for a short time. We need the money. What can I do, said Pepin — knock on her door every day? That is another problem. And there is no one to talk to about these things. Celso is older, cannot be there all the time, has not the energy.

I did not ask Pepin to explain the transaction with Chon. That is not my affair. He was explaining his anguish in trying to handle the administration of the farm and all the fiscal details while also doing the main work with the people there. It is necessary, I said to Manuel later, when Pepin was talking on the phone again, that there be someone who can manage the accounts and the administrative detail. It is hard to get a volunteer to do that. Someone should be paid to do that.

12:43 PM   The captain says: Folks on the right side can see Porto, Portugal. We have been cleared for our ocean crossing. Based on our time out of Madrid. and eight hours, five minutes flying time, we anticipate arrival in New York at 14:10 local time. For those that want to set their watch on New York time, it is now 6:43 in the morning.

3:17 PM   Flying. Over an ocean of clouds, a cloud of ocean. Vastness over vastness. Fastly over vastly. Smooth as silk, steady as she goes. And now — to *TIME*. Hey — maybe they agree with ME — the cover says "HELL RAISER, A Huey Long for the 90s, PAT BUCHANAN wields the most lethal weapon in Campaign '96: Scapegoat Politics." Scape that goat and apple pan dowdy. Read on.

4:58 PM   I just finished reading *TIME*. It took me — what? — about 1000 miles? But I walked up the aisle a few times, pee-ed — so my time wasn't all *TIME*. Now I am subjecting myself to a tyranny of the majority — and it probably isn't even a majority. Some people watch an idiot film and the rest of us must forsake the sun — close down our window shades, live in darkness, ignore earth and ocean and sky. It is crazy. As I write I push up the window shade. A blow for freedom?

TIME is not as bad as once it was. It no longer has MEDICINE, RELIGION, and so on. Has some fairly interesting essays. Has cut down on Gee-whiz-the-world-this-week-operates-anew-on-some-big-idea-our-people-discovered.   The last thing is a funny page by Garrison Keillor: "You go out to put salt on your sidewalk and slip, your arms waving like windmills, and something in your lower back twists loose, and you never attend the opera again. You spend the rest of your life in search of pain relief and wind up in India, penniless, lying on a mat at the Rama Lama Back Clinic, as the Master's disciple places the sacred banana on your back."

5:12 PM   My rear hurts, and I haven't done half the
sitting I must do today. Three more hours to New York.
Then St. Louis. Then Springfield, Missouri. I am to arrive
in Springfield at 4 AM Madrid time.   Ai, Ai.   I shall
now read *Businessweek* — the issue of November 6. The
TIME was October — oh no — I look again — the *TIME*
is November 6 also. Somehow, I looked at it before and
thought it was October 20, so I tore out the Keillor piece.
Well, November 6 is still two weeks ago. TWA must be on
the shorts. The *Businessweek* cover says "our first annual
buying guide — COMPUTERS — Hardware, Software &
Much More."

7:28 PM (1:28 PM New York time)   We should be
about 40 minutes from landing. I would feel great if
I were not going on from New York. But I have a night
of flying still ahead. NYC to St. Louis — with one-stop I
know not where. And then St. Louis to Springfield.

The pilot now announces we are near Boston and at
40,000 feet. He says we will land at 2:15. And the
weather looks better below than it was over the Atlantic,
where it was thick cloud. Here it is scattered clouds. And
dark land and gilded water come together below. Land,
sea and air.

7:51 PM   Bands of black, black-blue, white blue gold —
a strange aerial landscape — skyscape. But not bright —
the sun is now behind a cloud screen.

7:58 PM (1:58 PM NY time)   Coming down to the flat
fluff of the lower clouds, gold sheen on the water, a long
dark island.

8:01 (2:01)   Now under the lower clouds. The world here is soft grey, mysterious. The sea off to the left is gold foil. Now just below I see the long ridgelines in the sea. Water and cloud, glow and flat. Everything moves slowly, reluctantly. This big thing is searching for some place. Wavering this way, then the other. Nothing but water below. Oh, a shore, white surf, dark land — an island, a channel. We dip down, rock around. A watery land. Now I see houses, roads, a long sand beach, late Autumn trees. We move down, fast now.

2:11 PM   Down.

New York   3:53 PM (9:53 PM in Madrid)
On plane #2, which goes to Washington and then St. Louis. And it is now my bedtime. I feel it. My spring is about all unwound. But outside it is still bright afternoon. I called and reserved a motel room in Springfield, checked that Avis is still holding a car for me. I will stretch my way to Thanksgiving. I take my passport from my pocket and put it into my shoulder bag. It has lost significance.

Thanksgiving. I don't feel very thankful right now. I am tired. I just lost the nice ballpoint pen I bought in Jerusalem. But. I do have much to be thankful for. For the day and the light. Life and sight. That I have three seats all to myself. I shall try stretching out for a nap. On the Madrid flight I had two seats but I found there is no way to curl up and nap on two seats.

This is a supper flight. Question — is supper from here to Washington, or Washington to St. Louis? Must be after Washington, since it is not supper time now. We arrive in

St. Louis at 7:18 PM (8:18 Eastern time).

The stewardess says 40 minutes to Washington. We must stop for some time in Washington. This is a 727, it is less than a quarter full. So much for the busiest travel day of the year. Maybe no one goes to Washington for Thanksgiving? The stewardess seems cracker-jack — I mean good. I like the way she gave the safety instructions — she exudes confidence and competence.

I yawn. We taxi. There is a big white plane — a 747 — with the legend POLAR AIR CARGO inscribed on it. In front of us a big sky, a wide pale blue sky, an evening sky, and a few great grey clouds with white-rose tops. That's to be thankful for also.

4:18 PM   The plane sits in the far reaches of JFK. Lights of an incoming plane. Heading straight for us. No, he'll go over us. Now there is another one, just coming into sight. We aren't waiting for him. We move slowly forward. Then stop. The lights come closer, lower. Now they seem to be suspended. Heading straight for us. But, again, 60 feet up and just ahead of us. We are next for takeoff, says the pilot, so please be seated. Hey, we <u>are</u> all seated. Orange bright strip between the black clouds at the horizon — a beautiful color.

4:23 PM   Up up. Water, smooth and profound — not deep maybe, but profound. It is a waiting time. Right at the top of the circle. A changing time. Autumn. Day to night. Water changing to land.   The plane goes over on its side. I look down at water and an island of housely rectangles.   Now a puff of cloud alongside. Now above the white-wool clouds. It is all changed; we are sky people now. I see a coastline, a continent. The powerful evening sunlight — a golden-bright light — comes through the windows of the other side. A spot of sunlight fixes on the wall above my head. It is an orange light — very different from the cold light of the lamp above it.

I think of Madrid. Sitting in Celso's little house yesterday at this time of the day. In the little room, talking, drinking poleo tea. A simple, stable thing. And here I am sitting on a jet engine, moving with thunder and fire. Thunder and fire are very tiring. Poleo tea makes much more sense.

4:48 PM   I have moved over to the right side. The pilot says this is where we will see Washington. But dusk is coming on and there is a fleece of clouds below. He said we are going toward Baltimore and then coming up the Potomac past Mount Vernon. I crane my neck to look out the window a little behind me, for I am at the trailing edge of the wing and the window in front of me has a poor view.

What I see is patches of dark wooded areas, patches of clear areas. There's a river below. We leave Washington at 5:53 says the stewardess. Virginia below? No, probably Maryland.

I think of that woman at Esalen — when was that? 1990? She had a horse farm in Virginia. Came to Esalen. Wasn't going back.

Oh my, a great body of water below. Chesapeake Bay? A boat plowing the midnight blue water.

People change their lives, respond, struggle, fish about, do this fiercely, and then turn and do the other, also fiercely. It wasn't my way.

The plane slows. Now the left wing dips way over — we are descending to Washington. I still see only forest and clearing. Now buildings, a city, below. A river — the Potomac? The plane shudders. An electric motor — the wheels? Now over the river. City lights. We turn to follow the river.

Washington 5:08 PM   We are down. I see the lighted dome of the Capitol in the distance.

5:46 PM   Ready to go again. Now the plane is packed, every seat taken. It's coming on to midnight for me.

6:02 PM   Up again. A buzz of yellow lights below. Lights everywhere, auto lights, street lights, a sign on a tall building. Now, the lights thin out. We rise slowly, now dip and turn.

St. Louis   7:03 PM (St. Louis time)   Down again

7:43 PM   The next airplane. 3 AM in Madrid and I am flying the night away.

Springfield, Missouri   Thursday, November 23, 8:22 AM
Just a word. Awake, dressed, sunlight outside. Overhead, the sound of an airplane engine. My bag just fell off the dresser. We must never forget gravity — gravity doesn't take holidays.

8:56 AM   Well, I am sold on Missouri. Here, in this reasonably priced motel, is a good free breakfast. Cereal, English muffins, fruit. Comfort Inn North, Exit 8A of

I-44. Thanks be given to Comfort Inn North.

I think this morning of Julian Colby. How he lived, how he died. A guy to much admire. Did Iowa have anything to do with it (he grew up there)? Julian was a good person — was he also representative? Of a place, a time? Is breakfast at Comfort Inn North Julianesque? Fair, reasonable, life-enhancing?

~ *27* ~

Elixir Farm

Protected, sheeted, blanketed, humanized

Still Thursday, 5:03 PM   **Elixir Farm, Brixey, in the Missouri Ozarks**
The music at my ear, candles still alight. Peace at Thanksgiving evening. I am thankful. Gleam and eve and night coming on. I pick my teeth. We talk of walking up the hill to see the puppet show. Outside it is cold and colder. In here it is perfect temperature, perfect light. My arm muscles are asleep, my eyebrows are asleep, my calves are not asleep but immobilized. My stomach is working quietly, peacefully. The music plays on.

8:49 PM   Quiet. I am warm. The body is satisfied. I yawn. The quiet is so good. I hear real sounds, like the scratch of this pen across this paper, Peter pouring water into the sink. The sound in the house is of the house. In the city, sound enters the house, captures the house, stirs and roils the house. Enters the body, agitates. And the body defends. Clash, crush, commotion.

8:57 PM   To introduce myself: I am the one sitting on the white couch in Peter's living room. This is where the quiet is; this is where Thanksgiving 1995 happened. 1995 — or 1,995? 1,995 is the way it is given in the Feliz Navidad card of Escuelas para la Vida, which Pepin asked me to translate to English so they could put an English insert into those sent to foreigners.

At rest at Elixir Farm

Elixir Farm, Brixey   Friday, November 24, 6:11 AM
The dawning. Light gray and night gray. I write the way my sister used to read after my mother turned out the lights (and even took away the light bulb) — with a flashlight. I hold the little flashlight in my left fist, my hand closed over the light so only a crescent inch of light comes on the page.

Daylight comes on inexorably, for nothing can stop daylight, as nothing can stop night, or death, or rain or winter. It is quiet — the scratch of this pen, the crinkle of the page, the air coming in my nostrils. That's all.

Maybe there is some not-heard hum. A fan, a motor? My imagination? Now I see the branches, twigging out against the sky-gray light.

I think of the branches and leaves I saw against the sky — willow leaves — on the Vision Fast in September 1994 in the White Mountains of California. I don't have the same strong feeling now. Because I am not there, under the tree. I am here, inside, in bed. I am protected, sheeted, blanketed, humanized. The tree and sky are there — in the other world. The world past, the world to come.

I think of the Jewish formula for when Shabbat begins — for when the light is gone. It is when the threads of the prayer shawl can no longer be distinguished — is it one color from another?

6:31 AM   Lighter and lighter. I see two paths of light on the floor. Is this a reflection of a mirror, or some tall thin slit in the walls? I observe the paths of light. No. It is the two white fringes of the rug beside the bed. Shuffle and slip. Peter is coming down the ladder.

6:35 AM   More light. This page is clear, the writing not quite. The branches are black, solid against the sky. A whole tree against all the sky, digging down into the hill hump across the river. Rick's dog comes up on the deck, scratches lightly against the glass panel door.

6:40 AM   I lean in closer to the window, and can see the figures on my watch, the words on this page, without the flashlight. I feel the cold air. Not from the window. From the four-inch round vent over my head. My head is six inches from the books on the wall shelf. I read the titles on the spines. *Savitri* by Sri Aurobindo, and *A Life of the Author of the Raj Quartet* — I must lean very close to read that one. It is in a small script, yellow against dark red.

Another book: *A Tumult of Years*. Has to be an autobiography — interesting title. I pull it out to read the subtitle. It is a small book — an autobiography has to be a thick book. No subtitle. The cover design of the dust jacket is solid black broken only by the white letters of the title and, at the bottom, the author: Robert R.R. Brooks. That is interesting, the twin R R — but I never heard of him. I turn over the book — a photo, white on the black — a handsome head, white hair, thin face, creased forehead, confident smile. Underneath a paragraph: "The author has been, variously, an apprentice bookmaker, an architect . . . founder and dean of New Haven Labor College . . . Dean of Williams College for 17 years . . . written or edited eight books . . . lives in the house he built for his family."

Already I don't like him — and it probably is an autobiography — even without a subtitle and despite the size. A blast on the horn: here am I — notice me. Why don't I like this guy? Am I jealous of his accomplishments? Is he too self-satisfied? I will look inside.

Oh — someone has been reading it — the front flap of the dust jacket is stuck in between pages 86 and 87. The inside flap has a blurb beginning "This is a unique book by an unusual person . . . included among these stories covering 65 years, are descriptions of the mating of a Jersey cow in a Vermont pasture . . . There are accounts of President Angell at Yale . . ."

I'll look at the opening paragraph. It is something, I would guess, about birth (on a frosty morning in 1893, blah blah). Well, I wasn't far wrong — but he was born in summer. It starts "July 21 was the biggest day of the year." No, he was already born — on the next page: "On July 21, 1914 we were fully loaded by 8 o'clock in the morning and James was just handing me the reins. . ." Hey — I read the next page. Not bad — this is the mating of the Jersey cow. Named Gloria in Excelsis: ". . . his phallus extended and dripping . . . Gloria was appalled and started for home . . . I was much impressed with the bull's prowess and it later added to my respect for those cultures which have chosen the bull as a fertility symbol."

Hey, not bad — an autobiography that starts off as cow pornography. I go on to the second short chapter, which starts "My father, James Brooks II, was a very unusual man. For his time, which began in 1872, he was superbly educated." I like that: "his time, which began in 1872" — I don't think young people realize that: that each of us has a time, that it doesn't go on forever, that this is not *the* time, but *a* time. I read the second chapter. The chapters are short, about three pages. Hey, this is not a bad book, nor a bad person.

I see the book is signed — a nice old-fashioned signature. Maybe this was one of Peter's teachers. I flip toward the end. A chapter called "Timor" on page 148 — was this fellow in the foreign service? I look back at the publication information. Copyright 1980. He was born in 1905. Is he still alive? Hope so. I like him now. Here is page 87: "From a brown paper bag, Fulton Louis Jr, drew out an old-fashioned chamberpot . . . Tell Mr. Chester Bowles, he said, that this is a proper container for everything you have said."

10:26 AM   After. Breakfast, washing dishes. Still quiet. The quiet abides. It is solid and tangible. A very present absence. Or is silence an absence? Of noise. Maybe noise is the absence. Of silence. Of something powerful and natural, solid and present. Only when you live in unending noise do you think of silence as the absence of noise. Because you don't know silence.

Returning from woods walk with Pratt and Peter

12:39 PM   Sitting. On the white couch — in the warmth, protected from the outside cold. Talking to Peter in a rambling comfortable way.

5:15 PM   In from the cold. From a woods walk with Peter and Pratt.

10:57 PM   And so to bed. Cozy on a cold night — for which I am thankful.

✎ *28* ✎

More Elixir

The quiet gets into my head and I began to chatter.

Elixir Farm, Brixey **Saturday, November 25,**
6:46 AM

Birds. Caw, Caw, Caaaw. Light. No action. Quiescence, quiet. Colors in the light. Quiet colors: brown, tan, maroon. Warmth. Don't forget warmth. It doesn't come with the time and the territory. It is acquired, provided. By decayed forests in steel bottles, and other devices. Is that it? Well, to the best of my meager understanding. Shuffle and shift and crack creak. Humans join the birds. Making human sounds. The morning will take hold, grow into conscious day.

Last night, I woke at 3:59 AM and put on pants, shirt (no buttoning), sweater, socks, shoes — and walked out on the deck, swam out into the ice air — and pee-ed onto the leaves of Autumn past. After that I came back in, not chilled.

And when out, I looked up at heaven above with my near-seeing eyes. Yes, I saw several billion miles and more — but not well. The stars were mushed out. But spectacular when mushed. So what would they be smack crisp and jewel-like? I saw the dipper over the hill across the river. That's the only formation that stepped in and said Howdy Ralph, you know me.

Actually none of them were on a first name speaking basis. Nor was the tree. The leaves spoke a bit but that was because I gave my warm piss to them.

And I came in and lay down in this boat-shaped bed. An American mummy crossing the frozen hills of time. In the eternal ship. And the ship does, of course, move at incredible speed across the time of hills, rivers, bare trees. Among the stars, in a tiny baby-step way. If you get far enough away from slow-moving things like automobiles and radio music, you begin to feel the motion.

It is a soundless sightless motion and it carries all our toys, toxins and tempests along. That's why it's so hard to realize it. That is something to be awed by. But it isn't manageable. You may throw yourself out the window when you come into awareness of that kind of thing. And you are free falling — coming from nowhere, going nowhere.

I have no idea what I am talking of. The quiet gets into my head and I began to chatter. Though, I did falsify the caw, I think — it is caw caw caw caw caw — not caw caw caaaw. I heard it when I first woke and haven't since.

7:13 AM   No definite sounds of waking yet. So I reach back, without looking, to the shelf behind the bed. The first book is fat. I don't want a fat book. The dust jacket feels frayed. I turn my head. *A Pattern Language*. No. I reach again. A slim book. Pull it out. Set it on the bed cover, in front of me. *Such Times*, Christopher Coe. Grey and white. Back of a naked man. The bookmark placed in it has signs: ♀♀ ♀ ⚥ This I take as lesbian couple on the left, gay couple on the right. What is that in the middle? Hmmm. Transsexual? Both female and male.

The only digression from gray and white on the book's cover is the little orange circle with the penguin inside — in the upper left corner. At the bottom of the cover is "The novel of the decade. Treasure it" — *The Philadelphia Inquirer.* Hmmm. Philadelphia also says Proclaim Liberty Throughout the Land and to All the Inhabitants Thereof. From Leviticus. I turn the book over. Wow: "Wrenching . . . powerfully effective" — *San Francisco Chronicle.* "A fresh classic from the most elegant pen on the planet" — Paul Rudnick. "Perhaps the great novel of the AIDS epidemic" — Daniel Levitt. "Gives voice to the dreams and terrors of an entire generation" — *The New York Times Book Review.* "The gay novel of the decade" — *Publishers Weekly.* "A new classic" — *The Washington Blade.*

Well. So. Hmmm. I open the cover. Three more pages of quotes. The next page says "Christopher Coe grew up in San Francisco and lived in New York City. His first novel, *I Look Divine*, was published in 1987. Mr. Coe died of AIDS-related complications on September 6, 1994; he was forty-one."

There are 11 pages then before the first page of text: blank page, title page, publishing information page, dedication page ("above all, to my doctor"), blank page, acknowledgments page ("For guiding me to a clearer understanding of the ways viruses and retroviruses work. . ."), blank page, a page with a quote from Isak Denisen: ("the Duke of Alba . . . a handsome and brilliant man, married a plain and simple-minded lady . . . he [said] . . . the Duchess of Alba must needs, in her own right, and irrespective of personal qualities, be the most desirable woman in the world."), blank page, a page that says "SUCH TIMES", blank page, a page that says "ONE", blank page.

The first two sentences of text are: "There may have been a day this year when I thought of him as dead right off, the first time he came to mind. Most days I think of him as though he were alive."

8:14 AM   Washed dressed shaved. I sit on the white couch. Over my head Pratt talks to Peter. Peter's clothes come down — gravity. Peter comes down — gravity and ladder. Sunlight is in the house — pow on the chair back, pow on the black concrete floor, pow on the white wall.

Morning light at Elixir Farm

5:07 PM I step outside on the deck to pee. Dusk. A white sycamore, bare lyre-branches lifted to the sky, a white crescent moon embracing itself.

Awe-some, I think. Then I think what does "some" mean in that word? I tried to think of something else with "some" in it. Mettlesome? Winsome? Does it mean like? I'll look for a dictionary. Ah, an enormous Webster's unabridged on the window seat. I bring it to the white couch with my right hand. My left wrist can't handle this weight. Ah — "some [AS —sum, from base of same] a suffix meaning like, apt or tending to (be), as in lonesome, tiresome" Hmm — why didn't I think of those two common words — lonesome and tiresome? The dictionary also has: " —some and some [AS sum.] a suffix meaning in (a specified) number, as in threesome."

Then I read about the word "some" which comes from the Greek *soma*, body, and is a combining form meaning body, as in chromosome. That is something to drive learners of English mad. Same spelling, but here pronounced SOHME — whereas the other some is pronounced SUM. Then I read the definitions for some, adjective, some, pronoun, and some, adverb. And somebody, someday, somedeal (archaic), somegate (Scottish), somehow, someone "someone gently rapping, rapping at my chamber door" Then comes somersault and after that something, sometime, someway, somewhat, somewhere, somewhile, somewhither, somewise.

I carry the dictionary back to the window seat. English back to the tribes. There is a wondrous thing. The expression of these complicated things. Not technology or science, but these things that come fresh out of the blood and jelly of our brains — the way the jelly twists — it's hardware rather than software. The human brain produces language — that's another awesome thing.

5:45 PM   I go out on the enclosed porch and take an apple from the box. Bite. An apple is like no other fruit. It is the structure, the crispness. You eat an apple and it re-orders your inside. Apple juice, it is said, has very little nutritive value. But the apple is not apple juice. It holds itself apart, it holds itself together. It is tightly packed, dense, yet dissolves under pressure. It is a metaphor for the whole physical world — seems solid but is really a system of attraction and repulsion. It is appropriate that Newton saw an apple fall. Eve also? Somewhere I read that the fruit Eve ate was not the apple. I wonder what the Hebrew word is — and what fruit it represented? I pick my teeth after finishing The Apple. Put the core in Peter's chamberpot compost holder, near the kitchen sink.

Elixir Farm, Brixey Sunday, November 26, 5:56 AM
Darkness before the darkness before the dawn. I lie in the maroon-scape bed. Around me it is grey, black, intimation of light. I hold the little flashlight in my left hand, my blood-orange fingers curled over the light.

I should tell where I am, although I can't see it now. It is long — I mean more than wide, upright, square and high. By square I don't mean equal dimensions both ways. I mean the angles, the changes, are square, not curved. The floor is smooth, almost polished, black, the walls are white and wood. The windows lift up high, except for the windows on the uphill side where the house sits in the earth — there the windows spread wide from side to side. Two levels, wide decks on three sides. Open to the outside and open inside, but at the same time nooked and crannied. The land falls gently to the river, 200? meters away. The trees scramble-reach for the sky. Ladder to the upper deck, purple-black formica counters, kitchen area and sink/toilet room, big Jacuzzi tub in the other corner, screened-in veranda on downhill deck.

Now it is winter, life has gone to the roots — all conforms to the pattern of the sun. Over the long time — the very long time, everything has settled into compliance and harmony. The trees are patterned to the sun, we are patterned to the sun. What is the sun patterned to? It is hard to say — the sun is so immense, dominant, over-powering here, it is hard to surpass it, place it, in its own immense context. Maybe, come the new year, I shall attend that class at the University — "Overview of the Universe". I have always admired that title — overview of the universe, universe of the overview.

6:36 AM   A bird outside — muted, distant.

6:41 AM   The crow calls, raven calls. Is it crow or raven? A yearning sound. With the morning, the light coming. All the years going by, gone by. Hurtling on, standing still. Which is it? But I am a part of it — whatever it is. There seems enough space here, enough quiet, that maybe one could get closer, figure out what there is to be figured out. Stop. Or harmonize with some inconceivable speed. Float. Or disintegrate. Something besides riding in an automobile and listening to radio commercials. Ai Ai, I think. Caw caw, says the bird. Out the glass door, past the screen porch, beyond the bare trees, there are peach clouds over the dark hills.

Click — the clothes come by gravity. Now Peter follows by ladder. No, it is Pratt. Knights of the Square Table. Sir Pratt takes a bath. Rosie, the white terrier, paces quickly across the screened veranda. As I look out the long glass pane of the door to the light of the veranda, it seems as if I am looking at a mirror of the light of the tall windows besides my bed, the boat bed.

7:11 AM   Now the sky beyond the screened veranda is white, coming into blue. Here is a vast quiet comfortable overview of the universe. How about the old Rabbi in Jerusalem? I think. What is his morning view — the old yellow stone, crumbling? crowded and noisy? I mean the Rabbi I didn't see — the one with wide-open awe-struck eyes — the one David said he would take me to. The one awed by every person he met.

7:56 AM   I go outside to pee. When I come in, here is Peter on the ladder. Peter descending.

8:16 AM   Day comes on, sunlight everywhere.

11:53 AM   Sitting on the grass of the field. A perfect warm-sun morning. Pratt has gone, Rick has gone. A fly buzzes by. I hear birds screeching down along the river. I take off my sweater. It's hard to credit that winter will come before summer. Summer seems just a couple weeks away. I see the white sycamore trees beyond the line of bamboo at the edge of the field. Since Pratt pointed them out, I see the sycamores.

12:09 PM   The wind is in the trees, the white sycamores shift and shuttle. And then the wind is somewhere else, I hear it. Something moving. It could be a river. It could be an expressway. It goes silent. Then comes again. A crow caws way off — away from the river. The bamboo bends and prays with the wind. Sun Wind Crow. A brown leaf lands in the grass in front of me.

Something is happening. I don't know what. Now the wind catches this page. A big brown leaf flattens itself against my arm, then blows on. Another, gracefully gracefully turning comes to the grass ten meters away. Now I see wisps of white cloud coming from the sky in back of me. Leaves of grass stir, the brown leaves whisk a little. A little black fly bothers in front of my head. I pick my nose. I brought along this book Peter recommends, *Profane Friendship* by Harold Brodkey. I am reading the first pages. I like the way he writes. He is coming back to Venice. Airplane. Motorboat from the airport into the canals. Walking to an old Palazzo.

My bottom feels cold — I reach down to see if my pants are damp. No, the grass is just cold.

I pick up a leaf. Leather brown, twisted, torn. I pick up a different one. Is it a maple leaf? It looks something like the Canadian flag. That's an awful back-ass way of knowing a leaf. Beautiful leather brown, scallops and points. I look at the other side, where the stems or veins are more prominent. There are three main ones going out from the stem, one straight up and one to either side. They don't branch — each of the three goes to the edge of the leaf, ending in a point. But from each of them come other veins that go out to the edge. The subsidiary veins go out in a staggered fashion — first to one side then to the other — though in one place on the central stem, there are two veins that start in almost the same place and go to opposite sides.

I would guess that each leaf is unique in its exact pattern. I also guess that the veins in my body branch out in a similar way.   I lean way back, almost lying back on the grass, and reach out my right arm to pick up another leaf. The same and different. A thin brown-black bug, almost half an inch long, with many legs, lands on this page.

9:30 PM   The day, in summary, before turning out the light: Long walk with Peter down along Bryant River and up Hurricane Creek, supper with Peter, Vinnie and Lida. *My Left Foot* on VCR plus acupuncture from Vinnie and — la piece de resistance: a UFO which was as real as Kansas in August, until it came closer, and developed a motor and airplane lights. Maybe I'll describe it more tomorrow. So to bed.

Peter, Ralph and Pratt at Elixir Farm

Elixir Farm, Brixey Monday, November 27, 6:11 AM
Again the sky, imperceptibly changing. Earth and sun in
stately dance. Silently. All that mass and all that speed
— and yet silent. But, of course, there are energies —
our ears are not designed for them. No "need to know"?
We sweep a little space. Apprehend a tiny fraction.
This house does sail with earth into the sun.

It certainly is a mish-mash of information we get —
stars, a ball of fire rising from the hills each morning.
Very strange and disparate facts, sightings, sensations.
Now we have arrived at the preposterous explanation
that it all comes from a pinprick in time and space. An
explosion. Apparent order based on whim or lunacy. It
does boggle the mind. But not enough. The mind clings
tenaciously to its moorings of apparentness. Where else
can it go? To cell-dissolving fear? Like the spaceship-
from-outer-space fear I experienced for an instant last
night. The whole ordered world disappearing before me.

Here, the light is admitted in orderly squares. There is
shelter. Warmth. Music. Food. Soft. Gleam. One is not
exposed to cold fury. No — no expression of fury. But
without mercy. It would seem so. Oh, one could find
mercy. Leaves and hickory nuts, animals and animal
skins, stones and bones. But it would take a heap of
scurrying about. I am not up to it — don't feel up to it. I
would find cold fury.

But now I do have to think of the hands hearts minds
— of all time — that made the down cover, the concrete
floor, the hot water and the hot water pipes. What a
mountain I sit on. Lie in. Sleep on. Ballpoint pens and
flashlights. Batteries. Paper. Don't disparage those

things. And yet, and yet. And yet what? Do you want to brave cold fury?

There is the sound of a distant crow. The crow does it. But I am not a crow. The crow seems complete, flies alone. I am a fragment — of a million years — a billion-part assembly. Not to be disentangled from the whole.

I sneeze. My nose is stuffed. My eyes water. Watership down. Some little agent has seized me. I shall pad out to cold fury, in my bare feet, putting on nothing, to pee.

6:49 AM   I did it. In only my underwear. And did not hurry. Listened to the caws of the crows. Saw the white sycamore's many arms reaching to the sky, the dark fringe of trees mixed with sky on the ridge across the river.

~ *29* ~

West to Santa Cruz

I dance around the peanuts

Still Monday, 1:18 PM   **Springfield, Missouri airport**

Seat 17F. A cold day in Missouri. Gray and cold. Snow in Denver, says the pilot. There are but 18 rows in this plane, so I am in the next to last row. This is a BAe 146. I don't know anything about the BAe 146 — even why the e is not an E. But I put plugs in my ears, because I am back of the engines. The plane is full. Turkey travelers, I suppose. An hour and 50 minutes flying time, says the stewardess.

1:35 PM   We are up. Brown land — approaching the clouds. The pilot said it would be bumpy at first, so I trepidate. So far, just a shaking. Now all is gray. Getting lighter. Aah — we break through to blue. I look forward. This plane has crumple-shaped wings — a bit unnerving at first look. I think the plane is built in England — or Brazil? I prefer England, Although their competence seems to have peaked in turn-of-the-century locomotives. When you come on an airplane through a jetway, all you see is the door. You don't see the wing shape, the number of engines, paint design. The upholstery looks a little dingy.

A little airplane-history fantasy goes through my mind. Flew Dakar to Madagascar for 15 years for Air France. Sat in a Sahara airport for six years.   Ah — clever tray-table. It comes out of the armrest. Since there are only two seats here behind three in the row in front, the pulldown trays wouldn't work here. I drink orange juice out of a clear plastic cup.

I think of transparency. How are things transparent? I thought of that yesterday while sitting with Peter at that pretty little pool in Hurricane Creek. Asking then — how is water transparent? How is it we can see through this dense material? And glass? Of course — air — we aren't even aware that air is there — it is not only transparent, but invisible. Invisible — what else is invisible? Spirits and sorcerers? Gods, devils, essence and ether? True meaning, true love?

I should tell of the UFO of last night. Now It Can Be Told. Little green men in the Ozarks? Why green? Why little? Why men? Well, it is the time-tested formulation.

Vinnie and Lida had left, I was searching in my shoulder bag for the diagram of how to drive to the airport. Then Vinnie is calling in the door: Come quick — we may be seeing a UFO. I ran for my far-sighted glasses and ran out with Peter.

I saw it while I was still on the upper deck — a bright yellow light hovering in the sky. The light seemed to me to have rays going out from it — that could be my bad sight. Do you see colors? called Vinnie. Well, maybe. It was mostly yellow, but maybe there were other colors. When we all came together at a flat clear space a little above Peter's house, the light turned and came straight toward us. Then I saw some red in it.

Ah — lunch, such as it may be, is being passed out. A plastic box is thrust to me. Ah — this is why the men are little and green — in space you eat croissant sandwiches and chocolate chip cookies.

So — when the hovering yellow light came straight at us, that was the moment of truth. Vinnie called to Lida, Come over here, let's all be together. And we were — four humanoids in a line on a grassy knoll of an Ozark hollow, awaiting Fate. I grabbed Peter's arm. Peter said, There are lights, like a plane. Then, I heard the sound — like a drone, could be a motor. But there was a moment — when all reality began to crack.

Awe before the ineffable. It is custom, habit, usage, familiarity that dulls us, that keeps us from awe. I had never before seen a bright yellow light hovering in a still and distant night sky. I've seen these massy cotton-wool clouds hundreds of times. I've seen the blazing ball of the sun thousands and thousands of times. Ai. Ai.

Hey, the windows on this plane have two window shades — one pulls down halfway, the other pulls up halfway. Why? Maybe this creates a comfort class out of tourist class. Tourist class has only one window shade, gets only one chocolate chip cookie.

2:52 PM   I look at the route map in the United magazine. This flight from Springfield to Denver is mostly over Kansas. If our flying time is one hour 50 minutes, we should land about 3:25 PM (2:25 PM Denver time) but my flight to San Francisco leaves at 2:41 PM. O.J. Simpson running through the airport. But that was long ago. O.J. is not simple anymore.

2:59 PM There's the announcement — descent, on the ground in eight minutes. No, the pilot contradicts her — on the ground in 25 minutes.

3:10 PM Pilot says we've been slowed by hundred-mile-per-hour winds, won't get in until 2:30 Denver time. That gives me 11 minutes to catch the San Francisco plane.

3:19 PM (2:19 PM Denver time) My goodness, now all the crumples have come down from the wing — rinkydink aerodynamics. And the ground below is snow white. Winter in the Rockies.

2:45 PM (Denver time.) On the airplane, which was due to leave four minutes ago. Again the last seat in the house — 28C. As I came up the aisle, I was conscious that these are real people, San Francisco people, the people you live with. Such a one am I. I mean one who thinks like that. San Francisco, pupik (navel) of the Western World.

Right across from me is the magazine rack. I take this week's *TIME*, this week's *Economist*. Next to the magazine rack is the toilet. Tout comfort.

3 PM Taxi-ing. Snow on the ground, but not right near the runway.

3:03 PM Up in the air, Junior Birdmen. Wing down

over the snowy fields. Up up bounce jounce. Into the white mist of heaven above. Steady steady whine the engines — steady steady — jounce jounce. Darker, still in the mist of heaven above. We are going nowhere, with sound. We sound, we go go go — and we stay still in the white mist. But now, lighter. Still in the white mist. Still. Still.

3:10 PM   Ah, more light. There is sunlight somewhere. I crane my neck to look out the window. The jet engine is about one foot from the fellow in 28A. This is a 727. Well, lots of brightness now — Ah Ah, there it is — blue sky. We are above heaven above. The wool clouds roll away south — to a better land we know — look away, look away, Dixieland. Now I can relax and let the pilot take over. Ah, the pilot talks — 66 degrees in San Francisco. The sun shines best over the sun-shine West.

I am going to re-set my watch now to California time. If I were learned, I would know the proper prayer for re-setting your watch. But. Let's see. Can I devise a proper ritual? Oh god and gods and rocky mountain highs, propitiate —

Ah, here, right in the middle of my ritual is The Cart. The Cartress says Waddaya wanna drink? Orange juice, I say. So — now I have orange juice and a foil envelope of Eagle Honey Roast Peanuts.

I shall sacrifice the peanuts in the ritual. Hmmm. How? I'll dance around them. In my mind. Physical dancing about would interfere with the line waiting for the toilet. Om Be Um Ba Ba Boom Baam. I dance around the peanuts. I take off my watch, set it between the peanuts and the orange juice. Om Be Bam Boo Boo Bam. I tear open the packet. I throw two honey roasted peanuts in my mouth. Chew them. Drink orange juice. Now I throw in another six or eight. On the altar — the ivory altar of the teeth. Gold and ivory — no expense spared. Very expensive altar.

The peanut is the groundnut. Represents earth, fertility, fecundity. The orange juice is the fruit of the earth. Represents fluidity, sun-tone and Vitamin C. Ho Be Bam Boo Boo Bam. I finish the peanuts, finish the orange juice, take an ice cube in my mouth, pick up the watch. Ho Be Bam Boo Bam Ho Be Bam. It says 4:30. I press the button. Press Press. Bam Bo. Now it is 2:30, I am in California.

2:43 PM (California time)   I read some earlier pages. I see I said that I thought of aspects of modern comfortable Jerusalem as Best American [see page 120]. I didn't get a chance to explain myself because the lecture started then. I meant more than the physical by Best American. I meant also a kind of open intelligent discussion. Cardoso, Brandeis, Holmes, Dean Acheson, George Marshall. And I begin to doubt that I know what I meant.

Another clarification: When I was on the train going up to Jerusalem, I was delighted to see, from the train window, a fresh streamlet of water in the bottom of the valley [see page 54]. How delightful to see fresh water in this dry land; I thought it came from the rains of the night before.

I pause, take off my sweater; it is becoming warm in here. I rise, throw the sweater in the overhead bin. When I close the bin door, a tip of rosemary is caught outside.

But then, that afternoon (in Jerusalem), I had lunch with Fong, one of those from the ulpan in Netanya who had been with me on the train. I mentioned the little stream to him. Disgusting, he said, it is all sewage — an open sewer. So. That is why we must distrust scribblers and scribbling, as well as maintain a proper wariness on all reporting. What else did I want to revise? I can't remember now.

4 PM We are powering down to San Francisco. My bottom feels sore — it has been a sitting day. All going well, I hope to be home by 7 PM. Maybe I shouldn't say that when landing. Don't expect, don't anticipate. Break a leg. That's the thing to say. Break a leg. Should I do a ritual when I get off the plane? Oh my — I did it again. Anticipated. Presumed. Break a leg. Turn around twice, say Oog Booga and Break a Leg.

The pilot says, Prepare for landing please. I put up my table. I calculate this to be my thirteenth flight on this trip. Oy vey. But, as a Jew, am I supposed to be 13-superstitious? Doesn't it come from Judas, as the thirteenth for supper? Don't know. One of the hundred trillion things I don't know. I am hungry, I realize. I meant to eat one of Petey's apples, but I forgot.

The airplane now settles into a calmer stance. We must be coming up the Bay toward the airport. I can't see below from this seat. Oh my, is that the ocean I see — silver gold — or is it clouds? I do think it is the vasty Pacific. So. As the plane lands, my mind hears a lusty chorus of California Here I Come — to the accompaniment of jet screech. Down and down. Touchdown. 4:13 PM Someone in the cabin claps. My heart goes jig a jag

6:52 PM   Santa Cruz.   Record the moment. I have
arrived home.

On Being Jewish

My parents were Jewish in the bone and in the marrow, but had little to do with Judaism as a religion. They saw in the religion a good deal of narrishkeit (foolishness), superstition and old ways they had left behind in Russia. Their extended family and friends all shared that viewpoint.

Both my father and my mother arrived in the United States quite young, traveling to siblings already in America and painfully leaving parents never to be seen again — my father in 1906 at age 16, my mother in 1914 at age 14. My father was from Krinik, a town near the large city of Bialastok. My mother's area I am not certain of and today I have no one to ask.

Their association with Jewishness in Los Angeles, where I grew up, was with their Jewish family, friends and neighbors. They belonged to Jewish organizations, they supported many Jewish causes. They spoke Yiddish (their native language — they did not know Russian) to each other only when they did not want me or my sister to understand. Their life was in America, becoming American, learning English, making a living, raising me and my sister.

Growing up, I had almost no association with Judaism, the religion. We lived in East Los Angeles neighborhoods (Boyle Heights and City Terrace) which were almost all Jewish. The kids at my grammar school were, I would guess, 90 percent Jewish, and some of the teachers were Jewish as well. I stayed out of school on the Jewish high holidays, but I never went to synagogue. We sang Christmas carols in school at the end of every year because that is what one did in America. I did attend a local Jewish afternoon school where I learned some Jewish history and culture and a little Hebrew.

After grammar school, we kids from City Terrace went to Woodrow Wilson Junior High School, where we were the only Jews. For me, it was a jump from warmth and friendliness to a Siberia of wartime (1942 to 1945) bullying. Wilson was also a high school, but I, like many other Jewish kids, managed to transfer to Roosevelt High, back in Boyle Heights. While in high school I joined AZA, a Jewish teen group. I also belonged to a left Zionist youth group, Hashomer Hatzair. But I entered no synagogues. Until 1995.

In 1995, Stephanie, my niece Diane's daughter, was 12, and she invited me to take part in her bat mitzvah; my part was to read a few Hebrew sentences. The bat mitzvah was part of the regular Saturday service at a synagogue in Palm Springs. I think that was the first time I attended a regular service in a synagogue.

I was impressed. The rabbi was a young fellow who gave a sermon that espoused policies I agreed with. I liked the recognition of stages of life during the service: the bat mitzvah itself — a rite of passage to adulthood, the care for those who were ill or aged, the remembrance of those who had died. Also, being a great respecter of books, I was taken with the respect and affection shown for the Torah scroll.

Later, in the summer of 1995, I visited friends in Missouri and encountered an acquaintance who had recently converted to Judaism. She was very enthused about the rather new-age group Jewish Renewal and

Zalman Schachter, its founder. She told me Jewish Renewal was about to have a conference in Colorado. On my way back to California I stopped in Colorado and went to the conference. There I met several very appealing people from Santa Cruz. On returning to Santa Cruz I joined the local group of Jewish Renewal.

Then, in October of 1995, I decided to go on from my meeting in Maine to Israel with the purpose of learning more about Judaism.

I would add this: I've always been quite interested in Jewish religion, culture and history. I took an interesting course at UC Santa Cruz some years ago on the Torah as literature. I continued Hebrew for two quarters at the University after my return from Israel. I was in the local Jewish Renewal group for about ten years and participated in the services and the holidays.

But I don't find myself drawn to religious observance. My thinking on religion goes this way: we humans are small, vulnerable and impermanent creatures who live amidst immensities of time and space and awesome, hard-to-understand forces and complexities. We desire understanding of it all, a measure of security, perhaps some manner of controlling it all. Also, since we must live in community to survive, we need rules of how we treat each other.

Out of these desires and needs and our wondrous imaginative capacity, I believe, come many concepts like one God or multitudes of gods and goddesses, heaven and hell, resurrection, reincarnation, and so on. They are great poetics and comfort and guide to many, but taking them as life-molding reality does not serve me well.

Of course, the culture and my upbringing guide me in my daily life, and the culture takes much from religion. I greatly appreciate the values I saw my parents live by (which I see as preeminent Jewish values) such as generosity, a strong belief in social justice, and a great respect for learning. I do find meditation practice helpful and I have participated in a Buddhist group for several years.

Three Rabbis, a Soldier, and a Philosopher

Brief bios — with thanks to Wikipedia

Abraham Joshua Heschel (1907–1972) was descended from preeminent European rabbis. Heschel studied for Orthodox rabbinical ordination, then received a doctorate at the University of Berlin and a liberal rabbinic ordination at the Hochschule für die Wissenschaft des Judentums.

In October 1938, when living in Frankfurt, he was arrested by the Gestapo and deported to Poland. Six weeks before the September, 1939 German invasion of Poland, Heschel left Warsaw for London.

He never returned to Germany, Austria or Poland. He wrote, "If I should go to Poland or Germany, every stone, every tree would remind me of contempt, hatred, murder, of children killed, of mothers burned alive, of human beings asphyxiated."

Heschel came to New York City in March 1940. He was on the faculty of Hebrew Union College, the main seminary of Reform Judaism, and then from 1946 until his death in 1972, he was professor of Jewish Ethics and Mysticism at the Jewish Theological Seminary of America, the main seminary of Conservative Judaism.

Heschel believed the teachings of the Hebrew prophets called for social action in the United States and he worked for African-American civil rights and against the Vietnam War.

At the Vatican Council II, as one representative of American Jews, Heschel persuaded the Roman Catholic Church to eliminate or modify passages in its liturgy that demeaned Jews, or referred to an expected conversion to Christianity. He believed that no religious community could claim a monopoly on religious truth.

In *Man Is Not Alone: A Philosophy of Religion* (1951) Heschel talks of how people can comprehend God. Judaism views God as being radically different from humans; Heschel explores the ways that Judaism teaches that a person may have an encounter with the ineffable. A recurring theme is the radical amazement people feel when experiencing the presence of the Divine. *God in Search of Man: A Philosophy of Judaism* (1955) is a companion book to *Man Is Not Alone*.

Meshullam Zalman Schachter-Shalomi (1924–2014) was a founder of the Jewish Renewal movement and an innovator in ecumenical dialogue. He was born in Poland and raised in Vienna. His father was a follower of a rabbinic dynasty founded in the early nineteenth century in the town of Belz in Ukraine. and had Zalman educated at both a Zionist high school and an Orthodox yeshiva. Schachter was interned in detention camps under the Vichy French and fled to the United States in 1941. He was ordained as an Orthodox rabbi in 1947. He later earned an M.A. in psychology of religion at Boston University, and a doctorate from the Hebrew Union College.

While studying at Boston University, he experienced an intellectual and spiritual shift. In 1968 he joined a group of other Jews in founding a havurah (small cooperative congregation) in Massachusetts. In 1974, Schachter hosted a month-long Kabbalah workshop in Berkeley, California. He eventually left the orthodox movement altogether, and founded his own organization known as *B'nai Or*, meaning the "Children of Light," a title he took from the Dead Sea Scrolls writings. Both the havurah experiment and B'nai Or came to be seen as the early stirrings of the Jewish Renewal movement.

In the 1980s, Schachter added "Shalomi" (based on the Hebrew word *shalom*, peace) to his name, as a statement of his desire for peace in Israel and around the world.

In later years, Shachter-Shalomi held the World Wisdom Chair at The Naropa Institute, and was among a group of rabbis who traveled to India to meet with the Dalai Lama and discuss with him diaspora survival for Jews and Tibetan Buddhists.

Shlomo Carlebach (1925–1994) was a Jewish rabbi, religious teacher, composer, and singer. He was descended from old rabbinical dynasties in pre-Holocaust Germany. His family left Germany in 1931. In 1938 his father became the rabbi of a small synagogue in New York City. Carlebach came to New York in 1939, and he and his twin brother took over the rabbinate of the synagogue after their father's death in 1967.

Although his roots lay in traditional Orthodox yeshivot, he created his own style, combining Hasidic Judaism, warmth and personal interaction, public concerts, and song-filled synagogue services. At various times he lived in Manhattan, San Francisco, Toronto and a cooperative community he founded in Israel.

Carlebach composed thousands of Jewish religious melodies and recorded more than 25 albums. Bob Dylan, Pete Seeger and other folk singers helped him get a spot at the Berkeley Folk Festival in 1966. After the Folk Festival he remained in the San Francisco Bay Area to reach out to what he called "lost Jewish souls" — runaways and drug-addicted youth. His local followers opened a center called the House of Love and Prayer in San Francisco, to reach out to disaffected youth with song, dance and communal gatherings.

His tunes became part of the prayer services in many synagogues around the world, changing the expectations of the prayer experience from decorous and somber to uplifting and ecstatic.

Yitzhak Rabin (1922–November 4, 1995) was an Israeli politician and general. He was the fifth Prime Minister of Israel, serving two terms in office, 1974–77 and 1992 until his assassination in 1995.

Rabin was born in Jerusalem to Ukrainian-Jewish immigrants and was raised in a Labor Zionist household. He learned agriculture in school. As a teenager he joined the Palmach, the commando force of the Jewish community of Israel. He eventually became its chief of operations during Israel's War of Independence. He joined the newly formed Israel Defense Forces in late 1948 and became Chief of the General Staff in 1964 and oversaw Israel's victory in the 1967 Six-Day War.

From 1968 to 1973 Rabin was Israel's ambassador to the United States. He became Prime Minister of Israel in 1974, after the resignation of Golda Meir. In his first term, Rabin signed the Sinai Interim Agreement. Rabin was Israel's minister of defense for much of the 1980s, including during the outbreak of the First Intifada.

In 1992, Rabin was re-elected as prime minister on a platform embracing the Israeli–Palestinian peace process. He signed several historic agreements with the Palestinian leadership as part of the Oslo Accords. In 1994, he won the Nobel Peace Prize together with long-time political rival Shimon Peres and Palestinian leader Yasser Arafat. Rabin also signed a peace treaty with Jordan in 1994. In November 1995, he was assassinated by an extremist who opposed the terms of the Oslo Accords. Rabin has become a symbol of the Israeli-Palestinian peace process.

Jiddu Krishnamurti (1895–1986) was an Indian philosopher, speaker and writer. His subject matter included psychological revolution, the nature of mind, meditation, human relationships, and bringing about radical change in society. He stressed the need for a revolution in the psyche of every human being and emphasised that such revolution cannot be brought about by any external entity, be it religious, political, or social.

Krishnamurti was born in India. When he was 14, he had a chance encounter with the prominent theosophist Charles Leadbeater on the grounds of the Theosophical Society headquarters at Adyar in Madras. He was subsequently raised under the tutelage of Annie Besant and Leadbeater, leaders of the Society at the time, who believed him to be a "vehicle" for an expected World Teacher. As a young man, he disavowed this idea and withdrew from the Theosophy organization behind it.

He said he had no allegiance to any nationality, caste, religion, or philosophy, and spent the rest of his life travelling the world, speaking to large and small groups and individuals. Many of his talks and discussions were published as transcripts, among them *The First and Last Freedom*, and *The Only Revolution*. His last public talk was in Madras, India, in January 1986, a month before his death at his home in Ojai, California.

List of photos and scribble sketches

Map 1: Locations in the United States

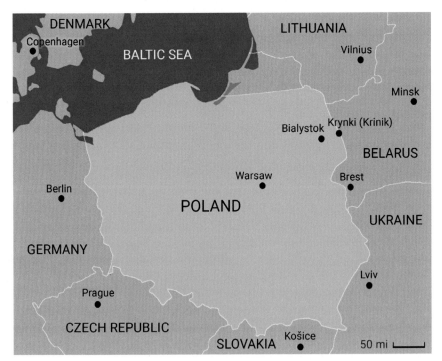

Map 2: Poland today, showing Krynki (Krinik), Mendel's hometown

Map 3: Israel

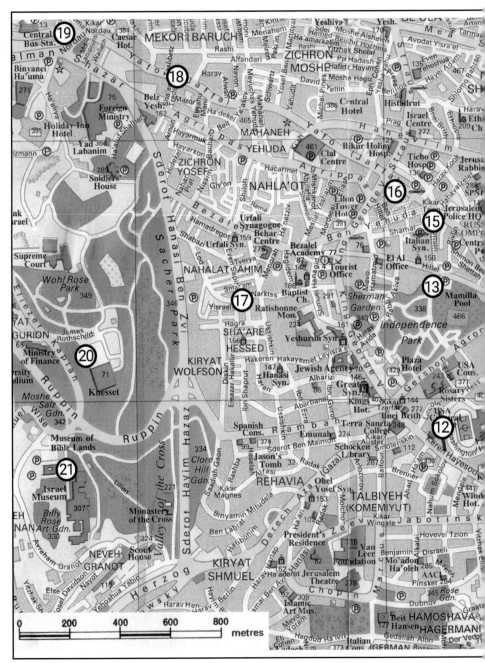

Map 4: Central Jerusalem showing Old City

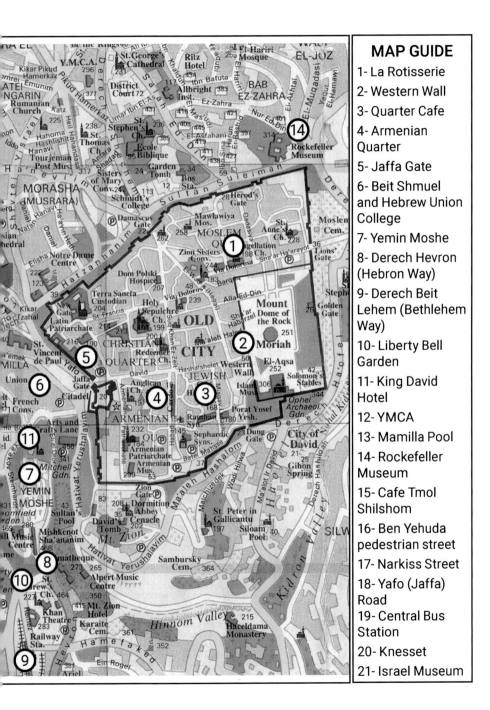

MAP GUIDE

1- La Rotisserie

2- Western Wall

3- Quarter Cafe

4- Armenian Quarter

5- Jaffa Gate

6- Beit Shmuel and Hebrew Union College

7- Yemin Moshe

8- Derech Hevron (Hebron Way)

9- Derech Beit Lehem (Bethlehem Way)

10- Liberty Bell Garden

11- King David Hotel

12- YMCA

13- Mamilla Pool

14- Rockefeller Museum

15- Cafe Tmol Shilshom

16- Ben Yehuda pedestrian street

17- Narkiss Street

18- Yafo (Jaffa) Road

19- Central Bus Station

20- Knesset

21- Israel Museum

232

Map 5: Spain

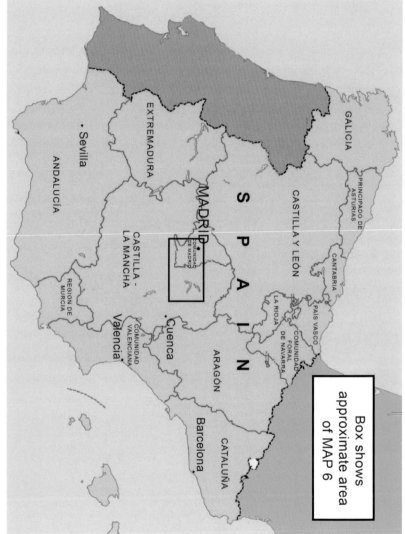

GALICIA

PRINCIPADO DE ASTURIAS

CANTABRIA

PAÍS VASCO

LA RIOJA

COMUNIDAD FORAL DE NAVARRA

EXTREMADURA

Sevilla

ANDALUCÍA

S P A I N

MADRID

COMUNIDAD DE MADRID

CASTILLA Y LEÓN

CASTILLA - LA MANCHA

REGIÓN DE MURCIA

Valencia

COMUNIDAD VALENCIANA

Cuenca

ARAGÓN

Barcelona

CATALUÑA

Box shows approximate area of MAP 6

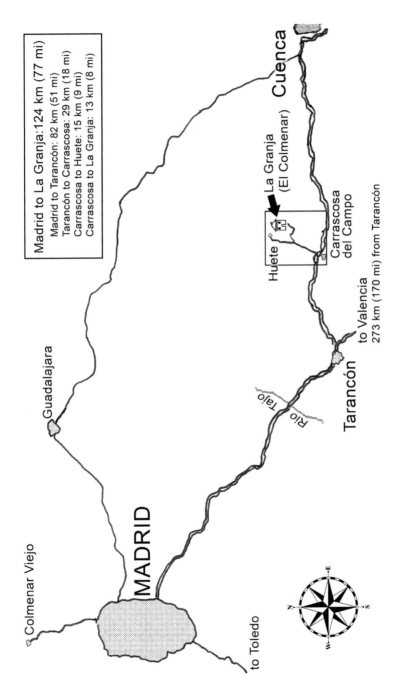

Madrid to La Granja: 124 km (77 mi)
Madrid to Tarancón: 82 km (51 mi)
Tarancón to Carrascosa: 29 km (18 mi)
Carrascosa to Huete: 15 km (9 mi)
Carrascosa to La Granja: 13 km (8 mi)

Colmenar Viejo

MADRID

Guadalajara

to Toledo

Río Tajo

Tarancón

to Valencia
273 km (170 mi) from Tarancón

Huete

La Granja
(El Colmenar)

Carrascosa
del Campo

Cuenca

Map 6: La Granja in relation to Madrid

Made in the USA
Lexington, KY
26 March 2018